# PROJECT REPORT WRITING

S.GEERTHIK
F.MOHAMED FAIYAZ
V.RAGHURAMAN
M.SINDUJA
P.VISU

Made with ♥ on the Notion Press Platform
www.notionpress.com

# Contents

# Contents

# Foreword

This book is prepared based on Anna University syllabus for the Subject Project Report Writing.

# ONE
# WRITING SKILLS

**What is Writing skills?**

Writing skills are the abilities to effectively communicate thoughts and ideas in written form. They encompass a wide range of competencies, from basic grammar and punctuation to advanced techniques like persuasive writing and technical communication. In today's world, strong writing is essential for success in both personal and professional life. Whether you're crafting an email, writing a report, or creating marketing materials, effective writing is key to conveying your message clearly and persuasively.

Effective communication is paramount in conveying the results and insights of a project. This book will explore the significance of strong writing skills in technical writing, particularly in the context of project reports. By employing clear, concise, and well-structured writing, project teams can ensure that their findings are accurately understood and valued by diverse audiences, including stakeholders, colleagues, and clients. This will delve into specific writing techniques, such as active voice, precise language, and logical organization, and provide practical tips for enhancing the overall quality of project reports.

**THE IMPORTANCE OF EFFECTIVE WRITING IN PROJECT REPORTS**

Effective writing is the cornerstone of successful project reporting. A well-crafted report is not merely a document; it's a communication tool that bridges the gap between project teams, stakeholders, and management.

- Clear Communication
- Decision Making Accountability
- Knowledge Transfer
- Professional Image

**Why is Effective Writing Crucial?**

1. **Clarity and Understanding:**

Clear Communication: A well-written report ensures that the key messages are understood by a diverse audience, from technical experts to non-technical stakeholders.

Avoid Misinterpretations: Clear and concise writing reduces the chances of misunderstandings and misinterpretations.

Knowing your audience is fundamental to effective communication. Tailoring your content and style to specific reader groups ensures your message is received, understood, and acted upon.

- Relevance
- Clarity
- Persuasion
- Tone

1. **Professionalism and Credibility:**

Positive Impression: A well-written report reflects positively on the author's professionalism and attention to detail.

Enhanced Credibility: Clear and concise writing builds trust and credibility with stakeholders.

3. **Decision Making:**

Informed Decisions: A well-written report provides the necessary information for informed decision-making.

Strategic Insights: Effective writing can highlight key insights and recommendations, guiding future actions.

4. **Accountability and Transparency:**

Clear Accountability: A well-written report demonstrates accountability for project outcomes.

Transparent Communication: Clear and concise writing promotes transparency and open communication.

## KEY WRITING SKILLS FOR PROJECT REPORTS

Effective writing is crucial for creating impactful project reports. Here are some key writing skills to focus on:

### Clarity and Conciseness

- Avoid jargon and technical terms. Use simple, direct language that is easy to understand.
- Employ active voice to make your writing more direct and engaging. For example, instead of "The report was written by me," say, "I wrote the report."
- Get to the point quickly. Avoid unnecessary words and phrases.

### Organization and Structure

- Develop a logical structure with a clear introduction, body, and conclusion.
- Use these to break up the text and guide the reader.
- Employ transitional phrases (e.g., "however," "therefore," "in addition") to connect ideas smoothly.

### Formatting and Style

- Use a consistent format throughout the report, including fonts, font sizes, and spacing.
- Utilize graphs, charts, and diagrams to enhance understanding and break up the text.
- Employ white space effectively to improve readability.

### Proofreading and Editing

- Check for errors in grammar, spelling, and punctuation.
- Remove unnecessary words and phrases.
- Obtain feedback from colleagues or peers to identify areas for improvement.

### Audience Awareness

- Tailor your writing style and level of detail to your audience's knowledge and interests.
- Maintain a formal and objective tone throughout the report.
- Ensure that your writing is accurate, fair, and unbiased.

## IMPROVING YOUR WRITING SKILLS FOR PROJECT REPORTS

Tips to elevate your writing skills for project reports:

### Deepen Your Understanding of the Subject Matter

- Ensure a comprehensive understanding of the project, its goals, and its impact.
- Seek insights from subject matter experts to gain a deeper perspective.
- Keep abreast of the latest trends and developments in your field.

### Master the Art of Effective Communication

- Tailor your writing style and level of detail to your target audience.
- Avoid jargon and technical terms that may confuse readers.
- Organize your thoughts logically, using clear headings and subheadings.
- Employ graphs, charts, and diagrams to enhance understanding and engagement.
- Pay meticulous attention to grammar, punctuation, and spelling.

### Enhance Your Writing Style

- Use active voice to make your writing more direct and engaging.
- Use strong verbs to create a more dynamic and impactful writing style.
- Combine short and long sentences to maintain reader interest.
- Connect ideas smoothly using transition words like "however," "therefore," and "in addition."
- Express your ideas clearly and concisely, avoiding unnecessary complexity.

### Seek Feedback and Continuous Improvement

- Share your work with colleagues for constructive feedback.
- Consider hiring a professional editor to refine your writing.
- Analyze your writing to identify areas for improvement.

- Study the writing styles of successful writers in your field.

By incorporating these strategies into your writing process, you can elevate your project reports to new heights. Remember, effective writing is a skill that can be honed over time with consistent practice and dedication.

**Examples of Effective and Ineffective Writing**

**Ineffective:** The project team was tasked with the responsibility of conducting a comprehensive analysis of the data in order to determine the most effective course of action to be taken.

**Effective:** The project team analyzed the data to determine the best course of action.

**Ineffective:** It is important to note that the results of the experiment were significant.

**Effective:** The experiment yielded significant results.

# TWO

# ESSENTIAL GRAMMAR AND VOCABULARY

Effective communication hinges on a solid foundation of grammar and vocabulary. Precise language is crucial in conveying complex ideas clearly and accurately, particularly in the realm of project reports. The essential grammar and vocabulary rules necessary for producing professional and impactful project documentation. By understanding and applying these principles, you can enhance the clarity, coherence, and overall quality of your project reports.

**Grammar**

- **Subject-Verb Agreement:** Ensuring correct verb usage based on the subject.
- **Tense Consistency:** Maintaining a consistent tense throughout the report.
- **Sentence Structure:** Constructing clear and concise sentences.
- **Punctuation:** Using punctuation marks correctly to enhance clarity and readability.
- **Article Usage:** Employing articles (a, an, the) appropriately.

**Vocabulary**

- **Precise Word Choice:** Selecting words that accurately convey meaning.
- **Formal Tone:** Maintaining a formal and professional tone.
- **Technical Terminology:** Using technical terms correctly and appropriately.

- **Avoiding Jargon:** Using jargon sparingly and explaining it when necessary.
- **Active Voice:** Employing active voice to make writing more direct and engaging.

## GRAMMER

### SUBJECT-VERB AGREEMENT

Subject-verb agreement is a fundamental grammar rule in English. It simply means that the verb in a sentence must agree with its subject in number (singular or plural). This ensures clarity and grammatical correctness in writing.

**Basic Rule**

**The most basic rule is:**

- Singular subject: Singular verb
- Plural subject: Plural verb

**Example:**

- The cat is sleeping. (Singular subject, singular verb)
- The cats are playing. (Plural subject, plural verb)

**Common Pitfalls and Rules**

Here are some common situations where subject-verb agreement can become tricky:

1. **Subjects Joined by "and"**
    - Usually plural: When subjects are joined by "and," they generally take a plural verb.
        - Example: John and Mary are going to the park.
    - Exception: When the subjects refer to a single unit or idea:
        - Example: Peanut butter and jelly is my favorite sandwich.
2. **Subjects Joined by "or" or "nor"**

- The verb agrees with the subject closest to it.
    - Example: Neither the teacher nor the students are coming today.

3. **Indefinite Pronouns**
    - Singular: Each, either, neither, one, anybody, anyone, everybody, everyone, nobody, no one, somebody, someone
        - Example: Each of the students has a book.
    - Plural: Both, few, many, several
        - Example: Many are called, but few are chosen.
    - Singular or Plural: All, any, most, none, some
        - The verb agrees with the noun following "of."
        - Example: Most of the cake is gone.
        - Example: Most of the cakes are gone.

**Benefits of Subject-Verb Agreement in Project Report Writing**

Subject-verb agreement is a crucial aspect of effective writing, particularly in academic and professional contexts like project report writing. Here are the key benefits of ensuring correct subject-verb agreement:

- Enhanced Clarity and Precision
- Professionalism and Credibility
- Improved Readability
- Stronger Argumentation
- Adherence to Academic Standards

In essence, subject-verb agreement is a fundamental building block of effective writing. By mastering this skill, you can create project reports that are not only informative but also impressive and persuasive.

**TENSE CONSISTENCY**

Tense consistency is a crucial aspect of effective writing, particularly in formal documents like project reports. It ensures clarity, coherence, and a professional tone.

**Why Tense Consistency Matters:**

- **Clarity:** Consistent tense usage makes the report easier to follow and understand.
- **Coherence:** It creates a logical flow of ideas and avoids confusion for the reader.
- **Professionalism:** Consistent tense usage is a hallmark of polished and professional writing.

**Common Tenses Used in Project Reports:**

1. **Past Tense:**
    - Used to describe actions or events that have already occurred.
    - **Example:** "The experiment was conducted on..."
    - **Commonly used in:**
        - Introduction: To provide background information or historical context.
        - Methodology: To describe the research methods and procedures used.
        - Results: To present the findings of the research.
        - Discussion: To interpret the results and draw conclusions.

2. **Present Tense:**
    - Used to describe general truths, facts, or ongoing actions.
    - **Example:** "The results indicate that..."
    - **Commonly used in:**
        - Introduction: To present the research question or hypothesis.
        - Literature Review: To discuss previous research findings.
        - Discussion: To interpret the results and draw conclusions.

3. **Present Perfect Tense:**

  - Used to describe actions that started in the past and continue to the present or have recently finished.
  - **Example:** "Researchers have shown that..."
  - **Commonly used in:**
    - Introduction: To summarize previous research or to introduce the current study.
    - Literature Review: To discuss previous research findings.

**Tips for Maintaining Tense Consistency:**

- Before you start writing, consider the overall narrative and the appropriate tense for each section.
- Avoid unnecessary shifts in tense within a sentence or paragraph.
- Stick to one tense within a particular section to maintain clarity.
- Carefully review your draft to identify and correct any inconsistencies in tense usage.
- Refer to a style guide (e.g., APA, MLA, Chicago) for specific guidelines on tense usage.

By following these guidelines, you can ensure that your project report is clear, concise, and professionally written.

**Benefits of Tense Consistency in Project Report Writing**

Tense consistency is a crucial aspect of effective writing, particularly in formal documents like project reports. It ensures clarity, coherence, and a professional tone. Here are the key benefits of maintaining tense consistency:

- Clear Communication
- Reduced Confusion
- Smooth Transition
- Logical Progression
- Polished Presentation
- Credibility
- Successful Submission

By prioritizing tense consistency, you can create project reports that are not only informative but also well-structured, professional, and impactful.

## SENTENCE STRUCTURE

Sentence structure is the foundation of effective writing. It dictates how ideas are arranged and conveyed, directly impacting the clarity and impact of your message. A fundamental building block of language, a sentence typically consists of a subject and a verb .Often, a sentence also includes an object

Example: The project team (subject) completed (verb) the report (object) on time.

**Common Sentence Errors**

**Sentence Fragments:** Incomplete sentences lacking a subject, verb, or both.

- Example: Running late for the meeting.

**Run-on Sentences:** Two or more independent clauses joined without proper punctuation.

- Example: The project was challenging we overcame obstacles and succeeded.

**Key Elements of Sentence Structure:**

1. **Subject:** The person, place, thing, or idea that performs the action or is described.
2. **Verb:** The action or state of being of the subject.
3. **Object:** The person, place, thing, or idea that receives the action of the verb.
4. **Modifiers:** Words or phrases that describe or qualify the subject, verb, or object.

**Principles of Effective Sentence Structure:**

1. **Clarity and Conciseness:**

    - Use precise language and eliminate unnecessary words.
    - Use active voice to make your writing more direct and engaging.
    - Vary sentence length and structure keeps your writing interesting and avoids monotony.

2. **Subject-Verb Agreement:**
   - Ensure that the subject and verb agree in number (singular or plural).
   - **Example:** "The **catis** sleeping." (singular subject, singular verb)
   - **Example:** "The **catsare** playing." (plural subject, plural verb)

3. **Parallel Structure:**
   - Use parallel structure to balance ideas and create a rhythmic flow.
   - **Example:** "She **likes** to **read**, **write**, and **paint**." (parallel verbs)

4. **Subordination and Coordination:**
   - Use subordination to show the relationship between main ideas and supporting details.
   - Use coordination to connect ideas of equal importance.

5. **Punctuation:**
   - Use punctuation correctly to clarify meaning and guide the reader.
   - **Example:** Commas, periods, semicolons, colons, and quotation marks.

**Tips for Improving Sentence Structure:**

- Expose yourself to diverse writing styles to learn from effective sentence structures.
- Practice writing to develop your skills and build muscle memory.
- Ask others to review your writing and provide constructive criticism.
- Grammarly and other tools can help identify and correct errors.
- Take the time to revise and edit your work to refine your sentence structure.

These elements and principles, you can create clear, concise, and impactful sentences that effectively communicate your ideas.

**PUNCTUATION**

Punctuation marks are the unsung heroes of written communication. While often overlooked, they play a crucial role in conveying meaning, clarity, and the overall tone of a text.

**Common Punctuation Marks and Their Uses:**

1. **Period (.)**
   - **End of a declarative sentence:**
     - Example: The cat sat on the mat.
   - **Abbreviations:**
     - Example: Dr., Mr., Mrs., Ms., etc.
2. **Comma (,)**
   - **Separate items in a list:**
     - Example: I bought apples, bananas, and oranges.
   - **Introduce a quotation:**
     - Example: She said, "Hello, how are you?"
   - **Set off introductory phrases:**
     - Example: After dinner, we went for a walk.
2. **Semicolon (;)**
   - **Connect independent clauses:**
     - Example: I like to read; my sister likes to write.
   - **Separate items in a complex list:**
     - Example: The guests included people from France, Germany; and Spain.

3. **Colon (:)**
    - **Introduce a list:**
        - Example: I need to buy the following: milk, eggs, and bread.
    - **Introduce a quotation:**
        - Example: The teacher said: "Please be quiet."
    - **Separate independent clauses:**
        - Example: The game was intense: the score was tied.
4. **Question Mark (?)**
    - **End an interrogative sentence:**
        - Example: What time is it?
5. **Exclamation Point (!)**
    - **Express strong emotion or surprise:**
        - Example: Wow, that's amazing!
6. **Apostrophe (')**
    - **Indicate possession:**
        - Example: The cat's toy.
    - **Form contractions:**
        - Example: Can't, won't, isn't.
7. **Quotation Marks (" ")**

- **Direct speech:**
    - Example: She said, "Hello."
- **Titles of short works:**
    - Example: The short story "The Tell-Tale Heart."

**Tips for Effective Punctuation:**

- Read your work aloud this can help you identify awkward phrasing and punctuation errors.
- Refer to a style guide like the MLA Handbook or the Chicago Manual of Style for specific guidelines.
- Punctuation should guide the reader, not confuse them.
- The more you practice using punctuation, the better you'll become.

Understanding and applying these punctuation rules, you can improve the clarity, readability, and overall quality of your writing.

**Benefits of Punctuation in Project Report Writing**

Punctuation is often considered a minor detail, but it plays a significant role in enhancing the clarity, readability, and professionalism of a project report. Here are some key benefits:

- Clearer Sentence Structure
- Precise Meaning
- Reduced Ambiguity
- Smooth Reading Experience
- Logical Progression of Ideas
- Visual Appeal
- Attention to Detail

By mastering punctuation, you can create project reports that are not only informative but also clear, concise, and professional.

**ARTICLE USAGE**

Articles are words that specify whether a noun is definite or indefinite. English has two types of articles:

**Definite Article: "The"**

- **Specific noun:** Used to refer to a specific noun that is known to both the speaker and the listener.
    - Example: "Please pass **the** salt." (Specific salt on the table)
- **Unique nouns:** Used with nouns that refer to unique things.
    - Example: "**The** sun rises in the east."
- **Superlative adjectives:** Used with superlative adjectives.
    - Example: "She is **the** smartest student in the class."
- **Musical instruments:** Used with musical instruments.
    - Example: "He plays **the** guitar."
- **Names of specific groups:**
    - Example: "**The** United States of America"

**Indefinite Articles: "A" and "An"**

- **Non-specific nouns:** Used to refer to a general or non-specific noun.
    - Example: "I saw **a** dog in the park." (Any dog, not a specific one)
- **Before countable nouns:** Used before singular, countable nouns.
    - Example: "I bought **an** apple."
- **Choice between "a" and "an":**
    - Use "a" before words that start with a consonant sound.
    - Use "an" before words that start with a vowel sound.
    - Example: "**a** cat," "**an** apple"

**Common Mistakes and Tips:**

- **Countable and Uncountable Nouns:**
    - Use "a" or "an" with countable nouns (e.g., book, pen, car).
    - Don't use articles with uncountable nouns (e.g., water, air, happiness).
- **Generic References:**
    - Don't use articles when referring to things in general.
    - Example: "Cats are domestic animals."
- **Proper Nouns:**
    - Generally, don't use articles with proper nouns (e.g., John, Paris).
    - Exceptions: "the United States," "the Amazon River"
- **Titles and Occupations:**
    - Use "a" or "an" before titles and occupations.
    - Example: "He is **a** doctor."

By understanding these rules and practicing, you can effectively use articles to enhance your writing and communication skills.

**Benefits of Article Usage in Project Report Writing**

Proper article usage is essential for clear and effective communication in project report writing. Here are some key benefits:

- Precise Meaning
- Smooth Reading Experience
- Attention to Detail
- Credibility
- Positive Impression
- Adherence to Academic Standards:
- Academic Rigor
- Successful Submission

Article usage, you can create project reports that are not only informative but also clear, concise, and professional.

**VOCABULARY**

Vocabulary, the lexicon of a language, is the cornerstone of effective communication. It encompasses the words we use to express thoughts, ideas, and emotions. A robust vocabulary allows us to articulate complex concepts with precision and nuance, enhancing our ability to persuade, inform, and inspire. Whether it's the everyday lexicon used in casual conversation or the specialized jargon employed in academic or professional settings, vocabulary plays a pivotal role in shaping our interactions and understanding of the world.

**Choosing the Right Words**

Effective vocabulary is crucial for clear and precise communication in project reports.

**Specificity:** Use precise words to convey exact meanings. Avoid vague or general terms.

- Example: Instead of "a lot of data," use "a substantial volume of data."

**Conciseness:** Choose words that efficiently express your ideas. Avoid unnecessary wordiness.

- Example: Instead of "in order to," use "to."

**Formal Tone:** Maintain a formal and objective style. Avoid colloquialisms and contractions.

How to **Build Your Vocabulary**

- Read widely: Expand your vocabulary by reading diverse materials.
- Use a thesaurus: Explore synonyms and antonyms to find the perfect word.
- Practice writing: Regular writing helps you incorporate new words into your vocabulary.

**PRECISE WORD CHOICE**

Precise word choice is a crucial element in crafting effective project reports. It ensures clarity, conciseness, and professionalism. Here's how precise word choice benefits your project report, along with examples:

**Benefits of Precise Word Choice in project report writing**

1. **Enhanced Clarity and Understanding:**

- Precise words eliminate ambiguity and confusion, ensuring that your message is understood clearly.
- Specific language minimizes the chances of readers misinterpreting your findings or recommendations.

**Example**:

- Vague: "The results were positive."
- Precise: "The results demonstrated a significant improvement in performance."

2. **Increased Impact and Persuasiveness:**

- Well-chosen words can strengthen your arguments and make your points more compelling.
- Vivid and descriptive language can engage the reader and persuade them to accept your conclusions.

**Example:**

- Vague: "The software was good."
- Precise: "The software exhibited exceptional efficiency and user-friendliness."

3. **Professionalism and Credibility**:

- Using precise language demonstrates a keen eye for detail and a commitment to quality.
- It enhances your credibility as a researcher or analyst.
- Well-written reports with precise language create a positive impression on the reader.

**Tips for Effective Word Choice in Project Reports**

1. **Avoid Vague Language:**

- Instead of using general terms like "good" or "bad," use more specific words like "excellent," "superior," "poor," or "terrible."

2. **Use Strong Verbs:**
    - Strong verbs add energy and vitality to your writing.
    - For example, instead of saying "The results showed," you could say "The results indicated."
3. **Be Mindful of Connotations:**
    - Choose words that align with the tone and purpose of your report.
4. **Use Concrete Language:**
    - Concrete language appeals to the senses and creates a vivid picture in the reader's mind.
5. **Vary Your Vocabulary:**
    - A diverse vocabulary allows you to express yourself in a variety of ways.
6. **Proofread Carefully:**
    - Review your report to ensure that you have used the most precise words.

Using precise word choice, you can create project reports that are not only informative but also engaging, persuasive, and professional.

**FORMAL TONE**

A formal tone is essential in project report writing, as it conveys professionalism, credibility, and respect for the reader. It involves using specific language techniques and avoiding informal or casual language.

**Key Characteristics of a Formal Tone:**

1. **Formal Language:**
    - Use the full form of words (e.g., "cannot" instead of "can't").
    - Use standard English.
    - Choose words carefully to convey your meaning accurately.

2. **Objective and Impersonal:**

    - Use third-person pronouns like "he," "she," "it," or "they" instead of "I" or "you."
    - Present information objectively and avoid expressing personal opinions.

3. **Clear and Concise:**

    - Avoid unnecessary words and complex sentence structures.
    - Get to the point quickly and efficiently.

4. **Correct Grammar and Punctuation:**

    - Check for errors in grammar, punctuation, and spelling.
    - Adhere to a specific style guide (e.g., APA, MLA, Chicago) to ensure consistency.

**Example of Formal and Informal Tone:**
**Informal:** "The software kind of crashed a lot."
**Formal:** "The software experienced frequent system failures."
**Tips for Maintaining a Formal Tone:**

- This can help you identify informal language and awkward phrasing.
- A thesaurus can help you find more formal synonyms for informal words.
- Ask a colleague or mentor to review your work and provide feedback.
- The more you practice writing in a formal tone, the better you will become.

These guidelines, you can maintain a formal and professional tone in your project report, ensuring that your work is respected and valued.

**Benefits of Using Formal and Informal Tone in Project Report Writing**

While formal tone is the standard for most project reports, there are situations where a more informal tone can be beneficial. Let's explore the benefits of both:

**Formal Tone**

**Benefits:**

- A formal tone conveys professionalism and credibility.
- It helps maintain a clear and objective focus on the subject matter.
- It avoids personal biases and emotional language.
- Formal tone aligns with academic writing standards and expectations.

**Informal Tone (Limited Use Cases)**
**Benefits:**

- In certain contexts, an informal tone can make the report more engaging and easier to read.
- It can help establish a connection with the reader, particularly if the audience is familiar with the writer.
- An informal tone can be used to explain complex concepts in a more accessible way.

**Important Considerations:**

- **Audience:** The target audience should be considered when choosing a tone. A formal tone is generally more appropriate for academic or professional audiences.
- **Purpose:** The purpose of the report will also influence the tone. A formal tone is suitable for formal reports, while a more informal tone may be appropriate for internal reports or progress updates.
- **Context:** The context of the report, such as the industry or organization, can also dictate the appropriate tone.

In conclusion, while a formal tone is generally the best choice for project reports, there may be situations where a more informal tone can be used effectively. However, it is important to use caution and ensure that the tone is appropriate for the audience and the purpose of the report.

**TECHNICAL TERMINOLOGY**

Technical terminology is the specialized vocabulary used within a specific field or industry. Using technical terms correctly and appropriately is crucial for effective communication among experts and for conveying complex ideas to a general audience.

**Why is Technical Terminology Important?**

- Technical terms provide precise and concise definitions, avoiding ambiguity.
- They allow for efficient communication between experts.
- Using technical terms correctly demonstrates knowledge and expertise.
- When used appropriately, technical terms can clarify complex ideas.

**Using Technical Terminology Effectively:**

1. **Know Your Audience:**
    - Adjust your language to the knowledge level of your audience.
    - If using technical terms that may be unfamiliar to your audience, define them clearly.
    - Use technical terms judiciously to avoid overwhelming the reader.
2. **Use Technical Terms Correctly:**
    - Ensure you understand the precise meaning of each term.
    - Use technical terms only when they are necessary and relevant.
    - Avoid using technical terms simply to sound knowledgeable.
3. **Balance Technical and Layperson Language:**
    - Use a mix of technical terms and plain language to make your writing accessible.
    - Explain technical concepts in simple terms, providing examples and analogies.
    - Diagrams, charts, and graphs can help to visualize complex technical concepts.

**Example:**

Instead of saying, "The algorithm iteratively processes the data," you could say, "The computer program repeatedly works through the information."

**Original Sentence:** "The algorithm iteratively processes the data."

**Simplified Sentence:** "The computer program repeatedly works through the information."

By following these tips, you can effectively use technical terminology to enhance the clarity, precision, and impact of your writing.

**AVOIDING JARGON**

Jargon, or specialized language used within a particular group or profession, can hinder communication if not used judiciously. While technical terms can be useful for precise communication, excessive jargon can alienate readers and make your writing less accessible.

**Why Avoid Excessive Jargon?**

- Jargon can obscure meaning and make your writing harder to understand.
- It can alienate readers who are not familiar with the terminology.
- Overuse of jargon can make you appear pompous or pretentious.

**Tips for Using Jargon Effectively:**

1. **Know Your Audience:**

    - Adjust your language to the knowledge level of your audience.
    - If using technical terms that may be unfamiliar to your audience, define them clearly.

1. **Use Jargon Sparingly:**

    - Use plain language whenever possible.
    - Use technical terms only when they are essential to convey a specific meaning.

2. **Explain Jargon:**

    - Explain the meaning of technical terms in plain language.
    - Compare technical concepts to everyday objects or situations.

3. **Use Visual Aids:**

    - Visual aids can help to explain complex technical concepts.

**Avoiding Jargon and Clichés**

**Jargon:** Overuse of technical terms can hinder understanding for non-experts. Use clear and simple language whenever possible.

**Clichés:** Overused phrases can weaken your writing. Opt for fresh and original expressions.

**Using Precise and Specific Language**

- **Strong Verbs:** Use vivid verbs to create impact and clarity.
  - Example: Instead of "said," use "asserted," "claimed," or "explained."
- **Descriptive Adjectives:** Carefully select adjectives to enhance meaning without being overly flowery.
- **Nominalization:** Avoid turning verbs into nouns unnecessarily.
  - Example: Instead of "the implementation of the plan," use "implementing the plan."

**Example**

**Jargon-heavy Sentence:** "The algorithm leverages a neural network to optimize the model's hyperparameters."

**Plain Language Equivalent:** "The computer program uses a type of artificial intelligence to fine-tune the settings of the model."

**ACTIVE VOICE**

Active voice is a grammatical construction where the subject of the sentence performs the action. It's a powerful tool for making your writing more direct, concise, and engaging.

**Why Use Active Voice?**

- Active voice makes your writing more clear and easier to understand.
- It often results in shorter and more direct sentences.
- Active voice can make your writing more engaging and dynamic.
- It can make your writing more persuasive and impactful.

**How to Use Active Voice:**

1. **Identify the Subject and Verb:**
   - **Subject:** The person or thing performing the action.

- **Verb:** The action being performed.

2. **Place the Subject Before the Verb:**
   - This creates a clear and direct sentence structure.

3. **Avoid Passive Voice:**
   - Passive voice can make your writing wordy and less impactful.

**Example:**

- **Passive Voice:** The report was written by the team.
- **Active Voice:** The team wrote the report.

Be Mindful of Passive Voice: While there are times when passive voice is appropriate, overuse can weaken your writing.

Use Strong Verbs: Strong verbs can make your writing more dynamic and engaging.

- Example: Instead of "The report was completed," use "The team finished the report.

- us on the Actor: Highlight the person or thing performing the action.

Practice: The more you practice using active voice, the better you will become at it.

Active voice, you can elevate your writing and create a more powerful and impactful message.

**Benefits of Using Active Voice in Project Report Writing**

Active voice is a grammatical construction where the subject of the sentence performs the action. It's a powerful tool for making your writing more direct, concise, and engaging. Here are the key benefits of using active voice in project report writing:

**1. Clarity and Conciseness:**

- Active voice makes your writing more direct and easier to understand.
- It often results in shorter and more concise sentences.
- Active voice eliminates ambiguity by clearly identifying the subject and
- the action.

**2. Engaging and Dynamic Writing:**

- Active voice makes your writing more forceful and impactful.
- It keeps the reader engaged by focusing on the action and the doer.
- Active voice enhances the overall flow and readability of your report.
- **3. Professionalism and Credibility:**
- Active voice strengthens your arguments by emphasizing the actions and outcomes.
- It demonstrates your ability to communicate complex ideas effectively.
- Well-written reports with active voice create a positive impression on the reader.
- **Example:**
- **Passive Voice:** The experiment was conducted by the researchers.
- **Active Voice:** The researchers conducted the experiment.
- The active voice version is more direct and concise, making it easier for the reader to understand who performed the action.

# THREE
# PASSIVE VOICE

Passive Voice is a grammatical construction where the subject of the sentence receives the action of the verb, rather than performing it.

- In passive voice, the subject of the sentence is acted upon by the verb.
- Passive voice is often used in scientific and technical writing to emphasize the process or outcome rather than the actor.
- However, overuse of passive voice can make your writing dull and impersonal.
- Use active voice whenever possible to create more engaging and direct writing.

**Why Use Passive Voice?**

While active voice is generally preferred for its clarity and directness, there are specific situations where passive voice can be useful:

1. **When the actor is unknown:**
    - **Example:** "The window was broken." (We don't know who broke it.)
2. **When the actor is less important than the action:**
    - **Example:** "The experiment was conducted successfully." (The focus is on the experiment, not the researcher.)

1. **To avoid assigning blame:**

  - **Example:** "Mistakes were made." (This is less accusatory than saying "You made mistakes.")

2. **To create a formal or impersonal tone:**

  - **Example:** "It has been determined that..." (This can be used in formal reports or scientific papers.)

**How to Identify Passive Voice:**

A passive voice sentence typically includes a form of the verb "to be" (is, am, are, was, were, been, being) and a past participle.

**Example:**

- **Active Voice:** The cat chased the mouse.
- **Passive Voice:** The mouse was chased by the cat.

**How to Convert Passive Voice to Active Voice:**

1. Identify the subject of the passive voice sentence.
2. Identify the past participle.
3. Make the subject of the passive voice sentence the object of the active voice sentence.
4. Change the past participle to the active form of the verb.
5. Add a new subject to perform the action.

**Example:**

- Passive: The book was read by John.
- Active: John read the book.

Caution: While passive voice can be useful in certain situations, overuse can make your writing dull and less engaging. It can also lead to wordy and unclear sentences.

**Tips for Using Passive Voice Effectively:**

- Rely on active voice as the default.
- Consider the tone and clarity of your writing.
- Review your writing to identify and eliminate unnecessary passive voice.

The nuances of passive voice and using it judiciously, you can enhance the clarity and impact of your writing.

**Example of Passive Voice**

**Active Voice:** The cat chased the mouse.

- Subject: The cat
- Verb: chased
- Object: the mouse

**Passive Voice:** The mouse was chased by the cat.

- Subject: The mouse (receives the action)
- Verb: was chased (past tense of "to be" + past participle)
- Agent: by the cat (the performer of the action)

As you can see, the passive voice shifts the focus from the doer of the action (the cat) to the receiver of the action (the mouse).

**Another Example:**

- Active Voice: They built the house.
- Passive Voice: The house was built by them.

In the passive voice sentence, the emphasis is on the house, rather than the people who built it.

| Active Voice | Passive Voice |
|---|---|
| Subject + Verb + Object | Object + Be Verb + Past Participle + by + Subject |
| The cat chased the mouse. | The mouse was chased by the cat. |
| They built the house. | The house was built by them. |
| She is writing a letter. | A letter is being written by her. |
| They have finished the project. | The project has been finished by them. |
| The teacher will explain the lesson. | The lesson will be explained by the teacher. |

Enter Caption

**Benefits of Using Passive Voice in Project Report Writing**

While active voice is generally preferred for its clarity and directness, there are specific situations where passive voice can be beneficial in project report writing:

**1. Emphasizing the Action or Object:**

- When the process or action itself is more important than the person performing it, passive voice can be used to highlight the action.
  - Example: "The experiment was conducted successfully."
- It can help create a more objective and impersonal tone, which is often desirable in academic writing.

**2. Avoiding Personal Pronouns:**

- Passive voice can help maintain a formal and professional tone by avoiding personal pronouns like "I" or "we."
  - Example: "It was determined that..." instead of "We determined that..."

**3. Emphasizing the Receiver of the Action:**

- If the impact of the action on a specific object or person is more important, passive voice can be used to emphasize the receiver.
  - Example: "The data was analyzed thoroughly."

**4. Creating a More Formal Tone:**

- Passive voice is often used in academic writing to create a more formal and objective tone.

However, it's important to use passive voice judiciously. Overuse can make your writing dull and less engaging. It's generally best to use active voice as the default and only use passive voice when it's necessary to achieve a specific purpose.

**Common Misuse of Passive Voice**

The passive voice is often overused in project reports, leading to unclear and ineffective communication. Here are some common misuses:

**Excessive use:** Overreliance on passive voice can make the text dull and monotonous.

**Incorrect context:** Employing passive voice when the actor is known and important can obscure meaning.

**Overemphasis on processes:** Focusing on processes rather than actions can dilute the impact of the report.

**Negative Impacts of Excessive Passive Voice**

**Vague and Unclear Writing:** Excessive passive voice can create ambiguity, making it difficult for the reader to understand who is performing the action. For example, instead of "The project team conducted a thorough analysis," one might write, "A thorough analysis was conducted by the project team." The latter sentence lacks clarity.

**Weakened Impact:** Passive voice can weaken the impact of your writing by obscuring the agent of an action. Consider the difference between "The researcher discovered a new method" and "A new method was discovered by the researcher." The first sentence is more direct and impactful.

**Difficulty in Identifying the Subject:** Overuse of passive voice can make it challenging to identify the main subject of a sentence. This can hinder the reader's ability to follow the logical flow of the report.

# FOUR

# REPORTED SPEECH

Reported speech is a valuable tool in project report writing, allowing you to incorporate the words of others into your text without directly quoting them. This can be particularly useful when summarizing interviews, surveys, or other primary sources.

Reported speech is a way of recounting what someone said without directly quoting them. It involves changing pronouns, tenses, and time references to fit the context of the reporting.

- Reported speech is used to report what someone else has said.
- It is often used in project reports to summarize the findings of other research or to report the opinions of stakeholders.
- When using reported speech, it is important to change the tense of the verb and use appropriate reporting verbs.
- For example, "He said that he was tired" becomes "He said he was tired."

**Reported speech**

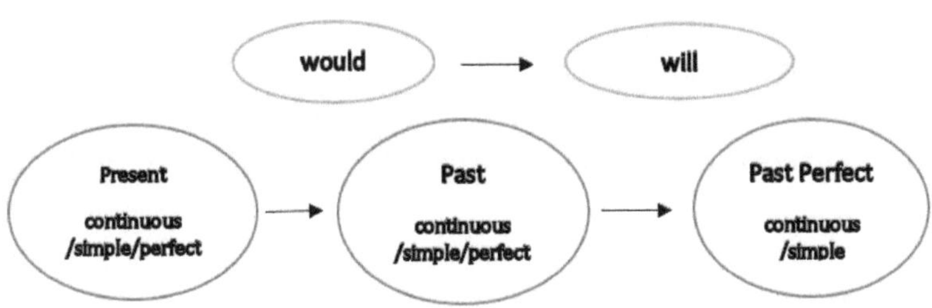

Enter Caption

## Most common Transformation

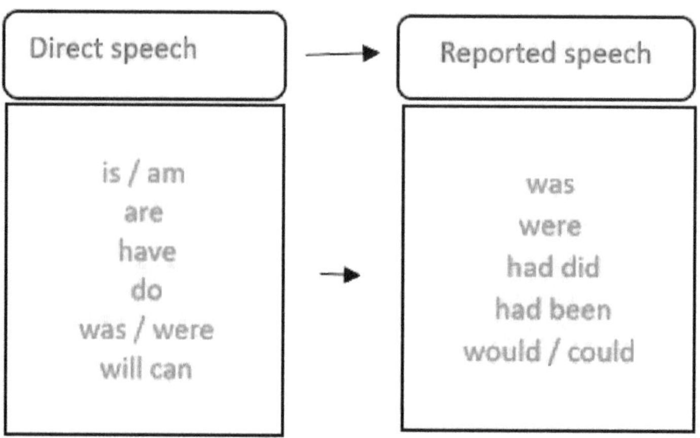


Enter Caption

**General Structure:**
**Reporting verb** (said, told, reported, etc.) + **that** + **reported clause**
*Example:*

- Direct speech: "I love ice cream," she said.
- Reported speech: She said **that** she loved ice cream.

**Why Use Reported Speech?**

- **To avoid direct quotes:** It can be more concise and less formal.
- **To summarize longer quotes:** It can help condense information.
- **To report conversations or news:** It's a common way to convey information.

**How to Report Speech:**

1. **Identify the Reporting Verb:**
   - Common verbs include: said, told, asked, replied, suggested, etc.
2. **Change Pronouns:**
   - Adjust pronouns to fit the new context.
     - **Example:** "I am tired," he said. → He said he was tired.
3. **Change Tenses:**
   - **Present Simple** becomes **Past Simple**
     - **Example:** "I like ice cream," she said. → She said she liked ice cream.
   - **Present Continuous** becomes **Past Continuous**
     - **Example:** "I am watching TV," he said. → He said he was watching TV.
   - **Present Perfect** becomes **Past Perfect**
     - **Example:** "I have finished my work," she said. → She said she had finished her work.
   - **Past Simple** becomes **Past Perfect**
     - **Example:** "I went to the market yesterday," he said. → He said he had gone to the market the previous day.
   - **Future Simple** becomes **would**
     - **Example:** "I will go tomorrow," she said. → She said she would go the next day.
4. **Change Time and Place References:**

  - **Today** becomes **that day**
  - **Yesterday** becomes **the previous day**
  - **Tomorrow** becomes **the next day**
  - **Here** becomes **there**
  - **Now** becomes **then**

**Example:**
**Direct Speech:** "I am going to the market today," she said.
**Reported Speech:** She said that she was going to the market that day.

- The reporting verb determines the tense of the reported speech.
- Pay attention to the context and the speaker's intention when reporting speech.
- Practice to master the nuances of reported speech.

These guidelines and practicing, you can effectively use reported speech to convey information accurately and concisely.

**Benefits of Using Reported Speech in Project Reports:**

- It allows you to present information objectively, without bias.
- It helps to clarify complex ideas and arguments.
- It can be used to summarize information without unnecessary detail.
- It strengthens the credibility of your report by citing credible sources.

# FIVE
# CONCORD

Concord refers to the agreement between different parts of a sentence. In project report writing, ensuring subject-verb agreement is crucial for clear and effective communication.

- It is important to ensure that the subject and verb agree in number (singular or plural).
- For example, "The team are working hard" is incorrect.
- The correct sentence is "The team is working hard."Other common concord errors include subject-verb agreement with collective nouns and indefinite pronouns.

**In English we find concord requirements in the following categories:**

- number: whether a constituent is in singular form or plural form
- person: whether a constituent is in $1^{st}$, $2^{nd}$, or $3^{rd}$ person form
- gender: whether a constituent is masculine, feminine or neuter

**Key Rules of Concord:**

1. **Singular Subject, Singular Verb:**
    - **Example:** The researcher **conducts** the experiment.
2. **Plural Subject, Plural Verb:**

   - **Example:** The researchers **conduct** the experiment.

3. **Collective Nouns:**

   - **Singular Verb:** When the group acts as a single unit.

     - **Example:** The team **is** working hard.

   - **Plural Verb:** When the individuals within the group act separately.

     - **Example:** The team **are** arguing about the strategy.

4. **Indefinite Pronouns:**

   - **Singular:** each, either, neither, one, anybody, anyone, everybody, everyone, nobody, no one, somebody, someone
   - **Plural:** both, few, many, several
   - **Singular or Plural:** all, any, most, none, some (depends on the noun phrase that follows)

5. **Subjects Joined by "and":**

   - **Plural Verb:**

     - **Example:** The researcher and the assistant **are** working together.

6. **Subjects Joined by "or" or "nor":**

   - **Verb agrees with the nearest subject:**

     - **Example:** Neither the professor nor the students **are** aware of the change.

**Why is Concord Important in Project Reports?**

- Correct concord ensures clear and unambiguous communication.
- It demonstrates attention to detail and adherence to grammatical rules.
- Grammatical errors can undermine the credibility of your work.

While concord is essential for clear and accurate writing, there are specific instances where it might not be strictly applied in project report writing:

**1. Collective Nouns as Singular or Plural:**

- When a collective noun refers to a group acting as a single unit, it takes a singular verb.
  - Example: The team is practicing hard.
- However, when the individuals within the group act separately, a plural verb can be used.
  - Example: The team are arguing about the strategy.
- In these cases, the choice of singular or plural verb depends on the context and the intended meaning.

**2. Indefinite Pronouns:**

- Indefinite pronouns like "all," "any," "most," "none," and "some" can take either singular or plural verbs, depending on the noun phrase that follows.
  - Singular: Most of the cake is gone.
  - Plural: Most of the cakes are gone.

**3. Creative Writing and Poetic License:**

- While project reports typically adhere to formal writing conventions, creative writing styles or poetic devices might intentionally deviate from strict concord rules for stylistic effect. However, this is generally not recommended in technical or academic writing.

**4. Regional and Dialectal Variations:**

- In some dialects or regional variations of English, there might be flexibility in subject-verb agreement rules. However, in formal academic writing, it's best to adhere to standard English grammar.

**Common Mistakes to Avoid:**

- **Subject-Verb Disagreement:** Ensure that the verb agrees with the subject in number and person.
- **Incorrect Use of Collective Nouns:** Clearly identify whether the collective noun refers to a single unit or individual members.
- **Misuse of Indefinite Pronouns:** Pay attention to the number of the indefinite pronoun and the verb that follows.

Remember to proofread your work carefully to identify and correct any errors in subject-verb agreement.

**Benefits of Concord in Project Report Writing**

- Correct subject-verb agreement ensures that your message is conveyed accurately and without ambiguity.
- Readers can focus on the content without being distracted by grammatical errors.
- Grammatically correct sentences create a smooth and easy-to-follow reading experience.
- It helps the reader understand the logical flow of ideas and arguments.

# SIX

# SIGNPOST WORDS

Signpost words are words or phrases that signal the direction of your writing. They help your reader follow your argument or narrative by indicating what's coming next.

- They help to guide the reader through the text and make it easier to follow the argument.
- Common signpost words include "however," "therefore," "in addition," and "consequently."
- Use signpost words to connect your ideas and create a logical flow in your writing.

**Why Use Signpost Words?**

- Signpost words help readers understand the structure and flow of your writing.
- They can keep readers interested by providing a sense of anticipation.
- They can highlight important points and ideas.

**Common Signpost Words and Phrases**

Signpost words are like road signs for your reader, guiding them through your text. Here's a breakdown of how to use them:

**Introducing a New Point**

- **Firstly, secondly, thirdly:** These words are used to enumerate points in a sequence.

- Example: Firstly, we will discuss the problem. Secondly, we will analyze the causes. Thirdly, we will propose solutions.

- **First, next, then, finally:** Similar to the previous set, these words can be used to indicate a sequence of events or ideas.
    - Example: First, we gathered the data. Next, we analyzed the data. Then, we drew conclusions. Finally, we presented our findings.
- **In addition, furthermore, moreover:** These words are used to add more information to a point.
    - Example: The new policy will benefit students. In addition, it will also improve the quality of education.
- **Also, besides, likewise:** These words are used to introduce similar ideas or examples.
    - Example: The company is facing financial difficulties. Also, it is struggling to attract new customers.

**Contrasting Ideas**

- **However, nevertheless, on the other hand:** These words are used to introduce a contrasting idea.
    - Example: The project was a success. However, there were some challenges along the way.
- **Conversely, in contrast, alternatively:** These words are used to present an opposing viewpoint or suggestion.
    - Example: Some people believe that technology is harmful. Conversely, others argue that it can be beneficial.

**Showing Cause and Effect**

- **Therefore, consequently, as a result:** These words are used to indicate a result or consequence of a particular action or event.
  - Example: The company cut costs. As a result, profits increased.
- **Because, since, due to:** These words are used to explain the reason for something.
  - Example: We were late because of the traffic.

**Providing Examples**

- **For example, for instance, such as:** These words are used to introduce specific examples.
  - Example: Many fruits are healthy, such as apples, bananas, and berries.
- **To illustrate, to demonstrate:** These words are used to provide a detailed explanation or example.
  - Example: To illustrate the point, let's consider the following scenario.

**Summarizing or Concluding**

- **In conclusion, in summary, to summarize:** These words are used to restate the main points.
  - Example: In conclusion, the findings of this study suggest that...
- **To conclude, to wrap up:** These words are used to signal the end of the text.
  - Example: To conclude, it is clear that...

By using these signpost words effectively, you can create a clear, well-structured, and engaging text.

**Example:**

**Topic:** The Impact of Climate Change on Coastal Cities

- **Introduction:** This essay will explore the devastating effects of climate change on coastal cities.
- **Body Paragraph 1:** Firstly, rising sea levels pose a significant threat to coastal infrastructure.
- **Body Paragraph 2:** Secondly, increased storm intensity and frequency can cause severe damage to coastal communities.
- **Body Paragraph 3:** Moreover, climate change can lead to coastal erosion, further exacerbating the problem.
- **Conclusion:** In conclusion, the impacts of climate change on coastal cities are far-reaching and require urgent action.

By using signpost words, you can create a clear and well-structured essay that is easy to follow.

# SEVEN
# COHESIVE DEVICES

**What are Cohesive Devices?**

Cohesive devices are words or phrases that connect ideas within a text, making it flow smoothly and logically. They help guide the reader through the writing and make it easier to understand. Think of them as the glue that holds your writing together.

- Cohesive devices are words or phrases that link sentences and paragraphs together.
- They help to create a smooth flow of ideas and make your writing more cohesive.
- Common cohesive devices include pronouns, conjunctions, and synonyms.
- Use cohesive devices to avoid repetition and create a more sophisticated style of writing.

**Types of Cohesive Devices**

There are several types of cohesive devices, each serving a different purpose:

1. **Reference Devices:** These refer back to something mentioned earlier in the text.
    - **Pronouns:** Replace nouns to avoid repetition.
        - Example: "The cat sat on the mat. It was purring loudly."

- **Demonstrative Pronouns:** Point to something specific.
  - Example: "I like this cake better than that one."

2. **Substitution Devices:** Replace a word or phrase to avoid repetition.
   - **Synonyms:** Use words with similar meanings.
     - Example: "The dog barked loudly. The canine made a racket."
   - **Antonyms:** Use words with opposite meanings.
     - Example: "She loves coffee, but hates tea."
3. **Ellipsis Devices:** Omit words that can be understood from the context.
   - Example: "She likes apples, and I do too." (Omits "like apples")
4. **Conjunctions:** Connect words, phrases, or clauses.
   - **Coordinating Conjunctions:** Join words or phrases of equal importance.
     - Example: "I like apples and oranges."
   - **Subordinating Conjunctions:** Join a dependent clause to an independent clause.
     - Example: "I will go to the park if it doesn't rain."
5. **Transitional Words and Phrases:** Signal relationships between ideas.
   - **Addition:** "also, furthermore, in addition, moreover"
   - **Contrast:** "however, on the other hand, nevertheless, although"
   - **Cause and Effect:** "therefore, consequently, as a result, because"
   - **Time:** "first, next, then, finally, meanwhile"
   - **Example:** "for example, for instance, such as"
   - **Summary:** "in conclusion, in short, in summary"

**Why are Cohesive Devices Important?**

Cohesive devices make your writing:

- They help the reader understand the relationships between ideas.
- They create a smooth flow and make your writing easier to follow.
- They help you build a strong argument by connecting your points.

**Guideline of using cohesive devices**

- Use Cohesive devices sparingly and accurately if you want to impress the examiner.
- **Example of Cohesive Devices in Action**

  Here's a paragraph with cohesive devices highlighted:

  The cat sat on the mat. **It** was purring loudly. **This** made the dog jealous. **However**, the dog knew **it** was not allowed on the furniture. **Therefore,it** just sat nearby and waited.
- Use cohesive devices appropriately and naturally.
- Don't overuse them, as it can make your writing sound repetitive or forced.
- Choose the right cohesive device for the relationship you want to express.
- By using cohesive devices effectively, you can create clear, engaging, and persuasive writing.

**Benefits of using cohesive devices in project report writing:**

- Cohesive devices help to connect ideas and create a logical flow, making the report easier to understand.
- Well-connected sentences and paragraphs improve the overall readability of the report.
- Cohesive devices can help to build a stronger argument by linking related points and ideas.
- The use of cohesive devices demonstrates a strong grasp of the language and writing skills, which can enhance the overall professionalism of the report.
- A well-written and cohesive report can leave a positive impression on the reader, which can be important for academic or professional purposes.
- In summary, cohesive devices are essential tools for creating clear, concise, and engaging project reports. By using them effectively, you can significantly improve the quality and impact of your writing.

# EIGHT

# PARAGRAPH WRITING

A well-structured paragraph is the building block of a clear and effective project report. It presents a single main idea, supported by relevant details, and transitions smoothly to the next paragraph. Here are some key guidelines for writing effective paragraphs in project reports:

**1. Topic Sentence:**

- The first sentence should introduce the main idea of the paragraph.
- It should be a strong, declarative sentence that grabs the reader's attention.

**2. Supporting Sentences:**

- Each sentence should provide specific details that support the main idea.
- Sentences should be arranged in a logical sequence, often chronologically, spatially, or by importance.
- Use transition words and phrases (e.g., "however," "therefore," "in addition") to connect ideas between sentences.

**3. Concluding Sentence:**

- The final sentence should restate the main idea or provide a concluding thought.
- It can also introduce the topic of the next paragraph.

**Example:**

**Topic Sentence:** The data collected from the experiment provided valuable insights into the behavior of the material under stress. **Supporting Sentences:** The tensile strength test revealed a significant increase in the material's resistance to deformation. Additionally, the impact test demonstrated the material's ability to absorb energy without fracturing. **Concluding Sentence:** These findings suggest that the material has the potential to be used in a variety of high-stress applications.

## PARAGRAPH LENGTH

### Ideal Paragraph Length:

The ideal paragraph length is a subject of ongoing debate among writers and style guides. While there's no strict rule, aiming for between 3 and 8 sentences per paragraph is a good general guideline. This range promotes readability and comprehension by breaking down information into manageable chunks.

### Benefits of Shorter Paragraphs:

- Shorter paragraphs are easier to follow and digest.
- Readers can concentrate on one idea at a time, reducing cognitive load.
- Shorter paragraphs can help to organize information more effectively, making it easier to identify key points.

### Challenges with Longer Paragraphs:

- Extended paragraphs can be intimidating and may discourage readers from continuing.
- Longer paragraphs can dilute the main idea by including too much detail or irrelevant information.
- Readers may struggle to quickly identify key points in longer paragraphs.

### Adaptability: A Case-by-Case Approach

While the 3-8 sentence guideline is a useful starting point, the optimal paragraph length can vary depending on several factors:

- **Topic Complexity:** Complex topics may require longer paragraphs to adequately explain the concepts.
- **Target Audience:** Less experienced readers may benefit from shorter paragraphs, while more sophisticated readers can handle longer ones.

- **Writing Style:** Some writing styles, such as academic writing, often involve longer paragraphs to provide detailed analysis and argumentation.

Ultimately, the goal is to create paragraphs that are clear, concise, and engaging. By considering these factors and experimenting with different paragraph lengths, writers can find the best approach for their specific needs.

**WHITE SPACE IN PARAGRAPH**

White space, the blank areas on a page, might seem insignificant, but it plays a crucial role in enhancing the readability of text. By strategically placing white space between paragraphs, you can significantly improve the visual appeal and comprehension of your writing.

**Why White Space Matters:**

1. White space creates a visual hierarchy, guiding the reader's eye through the text. This makes it easier to distinguish between different sections and ideas.
2. Excessive amounts of text without adequate white space can strain the eyes. By adding white space, you can reduce eye strain and improve reading comfort.
3. White space helps to break up large blocks of text, making it easier to focus on specific sections. This can be particularly important for readers with attention difficulties.

**How to Use White Space Effectively:**

- Ensure that the spacing between paragraphs is consistent throughout the document.
- Use appropriate margins to create a balanced layout.
- Choose a line spacing that is easy to read, such as 1.5 or double-spaced.
- Select a font size and style that is easy to read, and avoid overly complex fonts.
- Use headings and subheadings to break up the text and create a clear structure.

By incorporating white space into your writing, you can create a more inviting and reader-friendly document. Remember, sometimes, less is more.

## COHERENT IN PARAGRAPH

A coherent paragraph is one in which the ideas flow smoothly from one sentence to the next. This smooth transition is essential for clear communication and effective writing.

**Key Strategies for Achieving Coherence:**

1. **Use Transition Words and Phrases:**
    - These words and phrases act as bridges between sentences, signaling the relationship between ideas.
    - Examples:
        - Addition: furthermore, moreover, in addition, besides
        - Contrast: however, nevertheless, on the other hand, conversely
        - Cause and Effect: therefore, consequently, as a result, because
        - Time: first, next, then, finally, meanwhile
        - Example: for example, for instance, such as
        - Summary: in conclusion, in summary, to summarize
2. **Repeat Key Words and Phrases:**
    - Repeating key words and phrases helps to reinforce the main idea and create a sense of unity within the paragraph.
    - This technique can also be used to create a cohesive link between paragraphs.

**Example:**

- Without Coherence: The experiment was conducted. Data was collected. The data was analyzed. The results were surprising.
- With Coherence: The experiment was conducted, and subsequently, data was collected. This data was then analyzed, yielding surprising results.

## AVOID WORDINESS IN PARAGRAPH

Wordiness, or using more words than necessary, can obscure your message and make your writing less effective. By being concise, you can improve the clarity and impact of your writing.

**Strategies for Avoiding Wordiness:**

- Remove unnecessary words or phrases that repeat the same idea.
    - Example: "The reason why is because..." can be simplified to "Because..."
- Strong verbs can convey meaning more directly than weak verbs and adverbs.
    - Example: "The report was written quickly" can be revised to "The report rushed out."
- Avoid using phrases like "in order to," "the fact that," and "it is important to note that."
- Use specific language instead of vague generalizations.
- Carefully review your writing to identify and eliminate wordiness.

**Proofread Carefully:**

Proofreading is a crucial step in the writing process. By carefully reviewing your work, you can identify and correct errors in grammar, punctuation, and spelling.

**Tips for Effective Proofreading:**

- Step away from your writing for a short time before proofreading to gain a fresh perspective.
- Reading your work aloud can help you identify awkward phrasing and grammatical errors.
- Utilize grammar and spell-check tools to catch common mistakes.
- Ask a friend or colleague to review your work for feedback.
- Pay attention to areas where you tend to make mistakes, such as subject-verb agreement or comma usage.

**PARAGRAPH UNITY**

A unified paragraph is one that sticks to a single main idea. This means that every sentence in the paragraph should directly relate to and support the topic sentence. By keeping your paragraphs focused, you can improve the clarity and coherence of your writing.

**Tips for Creating Unified Paragraphs:**

- The topic sentence should clearly state the main idea of the paragraph.
- Each supporting sentence should provide evidence, examples, or explanations that relate directly to the topic sentence.
- Stay focused on the main idea and avoid introducing unrelated information.
- Transition words can help to connect ideas and maintain the flow of the paragraph.

**Breaking Up Long Paragraphs**

If you have a lot of information to convey, it's often best to break it up into multiple paragraphs. This can help to improve readability and comprehension.

**When to Break Up a Paragraph:**

- If a paragraph covers multiple main ideas, consider splitting it into separate paragraphs.
- Long, complex sentences can be difficult to read and understand. Breaking them up into shorter, simpler sentences can improve clarity.
- Long paragraphs can make your writing look dense and intimidating. Breaking them up can improve the overall visual appeal of your document.

# NINE

# TECHNICAL WRITING VS. GENERAL WRITING

While technical writing forms the backbone of a project report, incorporating elements of general writing can significantly enhance its readability and impact. It's about finding the right balance between conveying complex information clearly and engaging the reader.

**TECHNICAL WRITING**

Technical writing is a specialized form of communication that focuses on conveying complex information clearly, accurately, and concisely to a specific audience. It involves transforming technical and specialized knowledge into easily understandable content.

**Purpose**

- The primary purpose of technical writing is to inform, instruct, or persuade the reader about a particular subject or process. It aims to bridge the gap between complex technical information and the needs of the target audience, enabling them to perform tasks, make decisions, or understand concepts effectively.

**Example**

**Manuals:** These documents provide step-by-step instructions on how to use products or equipment. They often include diagrams, illustrations, and troubleshooting guides.

- Example: A user manual for a smartphone, explaining its features, setup, and troubleshooting steps.

**Reports:** Technical reports present findings, analyses, and recommendations based on research or data. They are often used in academic, scientific, or business contexts.

- Example: A research report on the environmental impact of a new technology.

**Proposals:** Proposals outline plans or solutions to specific problems or challenges. They often include detailed descriptions, budgets, and timelines.

- Example: A proposal for a new software development project, outlining project goals, scope, and deliverables.

## GENERAL WRITING

General writing is a broad term encompassing any form of written expression that doesn't strictly adhere to the rules and conventions of technical writing. It often involves personal expression, creativity, and the exploration of ideas.

**Purpose**

- The purpose of general writing is diverse. It can entertain, inform, persuade, or evoke emotions. The primary goal is to connect with the reader on a personal level and create a shared experience.

**Example:**

**Stories:** Fictional narratives that transport readers to different worlds, introducing them to characters and plotlines. Stories can be short or long, and they often aim to entertain and engage the reader emotionally.

- Example: A short story about a young woman who discovers a magical world hidden within her everyday life.

**Poems:** Expressive forms of writing that use language creatively to evoke emotions, images, and ideas. Poems can vary in structure, rhyme, and rhythm.

- Example: A free verse poem about the beauty of nature and the interconnectedness of all living things.

**Essays:** Non-fiction pieces that explore a particular topic or theme. Essays can be personal, analytical, or argumentative, offering the writer's perspective on a subject.

- Example: A personal essay about overcoming a challenge or a reflective essay on the meaning of life.

| Feature | Technical Writing | General Writing |
|---|---|---|
| Purpose | To inform, instruct, or explain complex technical information | To entertain, persuade, or narrate stories |
| Audience | Specific audience with specialized knowledge | Broad audience with varying levels of knowledge |
| Style and Tone | Formal, objective, and precise | Varies widely, from formal to informal |
| Structure | Highly structured with clear headings and subheadings | More flexible structure, depending on genre and purpose |
| Examples | User manuals, technical reports, research papers, software documentation | Novels, short stories, essays, blog posts, news articles, marketing materials |

**Importance of Technical Writing in Project Reports**

- Enhancing clarity and precision
- Improving
- readability
- Facilitating understanding
- Building credibility
- In essence, technical writing is indispensable for creating project reports that are not only informative but also engaging and persuasive. By adhering to the principles of clarity, precision, readability, and understanding, project teams can produce documents that effectively communicate their work and achieve their project goals.

By applying these design principles, you can significantly enhance the readability and understanding of your report.

- **Improved Comprehension:** Clear and well-organized tables and illustrations facilitate easier information processing.
- **Enhanced Engagement:** Visually appealing graphics can capture the reader's attention and encourage deeper engagement with the content.
- **Faster Information Retrieval:** Effective use of design elements helps readers quickly locate specific information within the table or illustration.
- **Increased Credibility:** Professionally designed visuals enhance the
- overall credibility of the report.

# TEN

# PROJECT REPORT

## DEFINITION

A project report is a comprehensive document that outlines a project's details, progress, and outcomes. It serves as a formal record for the management team, stakeholders, and future projects. This structured document captures the essential aspects of a project.

**Components of Project Report**

- Project progress
- Risk and Management
- Budget
- Timelines
- Team Performance
- Executive summary
- Conclusion & Completion

**The Primary Purpose of a Project Report**

A project report is a critical document that serves multiple purposes beyond merely communicating project status and achievements. It's a comprehensive record that offers insights, analysis, and recommendations for future projects.

**Key Purposes of a Project Report:**

1. **Documentation and Record-Keeping:**

- Historical Reference
- Legal and Compliance

**Historical Reference**

A project report serves as a time capsule, capturing the evolution of a project from its inception to completion. By documenting key decisions, milestones, and challenges, it provides a valuable historical reference for future analysis and learning.

- Details the rationale behind significant decisions, including the evaluation of alternatives and potential consequences.
- Records identified risks, mitigation strategies, and the effectiveness of risk response plans.
- Documents changes to the project scope, schedule, or budget, along with the justification for these changes.
- Captures insights gained from project experiences, both positive and negative, to inform future projects.

**Legal and Compliance**

A well-documented project report ensures compliance with relevant laws, regulations, and contractual obligations. It provides evidence of:

- Demonstrates conformance to industry standards and best practices.
- Verifies the fulfillment of contractual obligations, including deliverables, timelines, and performance metrics.
- Shows compliance with government regulations and industry-specific guidelines.
- Records ownership and usage rights of intellectual property generated during the project.

Maintaining comprehensive documentation, organizations can mitigate legal risks, protect their interests, and enhance their reputation for responsible and ethical project management.

1. **Performance Evaluation:**

- Progress Tracking
- Risk Assessment
- Performance Metrics

**Progress Tracking**

- Monitors the achievement of significant project milestones, ensuring timely completion.
- Tracks individual tasks and their dependencies to identify potential bottlenecks and delays.
- Provides regular updates on project progress to stakeholders, including status reports, dashboards, and visual representations.

**Risk Assessment**

- Identifies potential risks that could impact the project's success.
- Evaluates the likelihood and potential impact of identified risks.
- Develops strategies to minimize the impact of risks and contingency plans to address unexpected issues.
- Continuously monitors risks and updates risk assessments as needed.

**Performance Metrics**

- Defines relevant KPIs to measure project performance, such as cost, schedule, quality, and customer satisfaction.
- Uses quantitative data to assess project performance against established benchmarks.
- Evaluates qualitative factors, such as team morale, stakeholder satisfaction, and project innovation.
- Generates regular performance reports to highlight achievements, challenges, and areas for improvement.

3. **Decision-Making:**

- Informed Choices
- Resource Allocation
- Change Management

**Informed Choices**

- Using data and analytics to make informed decisions rather than relying on intuition or guesswork. This involves collecting and analyzing relevant data, such as project performance metrics, risk assessments, and stakeholder feedback. Making decisions based on evidence and facts, rather than opinions or assumptions.

**Resource Allocation**

- Allocating resources (human, financial, and physical) effectively to maximize project outcomes. Balancing resource demand and availability to avoid resource shortages or overallocation. Evaluating the costs and benefits of different resource allocation options to make informed decisions.

**Change Management**

- Identifying and addressing potential changes early to minimize disruptions to the project.
- Implementing a formal process for evaluating, approving, and managing changes to the project plan.

4. **Communication and Stakeholder Management:**

- Transparency
- Relationship Building
- Issue Resolution

**Transparency**

- Sharing project information with stakeholders in a timely and transparent manner.
- Providing regular updates on project progress, milestones, and key decisions.
- Using clear and concise language to communicate complex information.

**Relationship Building**

- Paying attention to stakeholder needs, concerns, and feedback. Using appropriate communication channels and methods to reach stakeholders. Demonstrating reliability, competence, and integrity.

**Issue Resolution**

- Identifying and addressing potential issues before they escalate.
- Using problem-solving techniques to resolve issues efficiently.
- Involving stakeholders in the issue resolution process to find mutually beneficial solutions.

5. **Future Planning:**

- Lessons Learned
- Knowledge Transfer
- Continuous Improvement

**Lessons Learned**

- Conducting a thorough review of the project to identify successes, failures, and areas for improvement.
- Creating a formal document to capture key lessons and share them with the organization.
- Sharing lessons learned with project teams and other relevant stakeholders.

**Knowledge Transfer**

- Organizing workshops, seminars, or training sessions to share knowledge and expertise.
- Providing mentoring and coaching opportunities to develop skills and knowledge.
- Creating a repository of best practices and lessons learned.

**Continuous Improvement**

- Analyzing project performance data to identify areas for improvement.
- Implementing process improvements to enhance efficiency and effectiveness.
- Encouraging innovation and creativity to develop new solutions and approaches.
- Establishing feedback mechanisms to gather input from stakeholders and project team members.

**Importance of Effective Project Report Writing**

- **Data-Driven Decision Making:** Making decisions based on facts, data, and analysis rather than intuition or assumptions.
- **Clear Roles and Responsibilities:** Defining and assigning clear roles and responsibilities to all team members.
- **Knowledge Management Systems:** Implementing systems to capture, store, and share knowledge and expertise.
- **Proactive Risk Identification**: Identifying potential risks early in the project lifecycle.
- **Effective Communication Channels:** Utilizing appropriate communication channels to reach and engage stakeholders.
- **Post-Project Review:** Conducting a thorough review of the project to identify lessons learned and areas for improvement.

**Few examples of introductory paragraphs for a project report:**

**Example 1: General Introduction**

This project report presents a comprehensive analysis of [project topic]. The primary objective of this study is to [state the main goal]. To achieve this goal, we [describe the methodology used]. The findings of this research will contribute to a better understanding of [the significance of the topic].

**Example 2: Technical Project**

This project report documents the development and implementation of [project name], a [type of system or application] designed to [state the purpose]. The system utilizes [key technologies or methodologies] to [describe the core functionalities]. The report will delve into the system's architecture, design, implementation, and evaluation.

**Example 3: Research Project**

This research project aims to investigate the impact of [independent variable] on [dependent variable]. By employing a [research methodology], we seek to uncover the underlying mechanisms and relationships between these variables. The findings of this study will provide valuable insights into [the significance of the research].

# ELEVEN

# STRUCTURE OF PROJECT REPORT

**[Title Page] --> {Abstract} --> {Table of Contents} --> {List of Figures} --> {Executive Summary} --> {Introduction} --> {Body} --> {Conclusion} --> {Recommendations} --> {Appendix} --> {Glossary} --> {Letter of Transmittal}**

**Standard Structure of a Project Report**

A well-structured project report provides a clear and concise overview of a project, its objectives, methodologies, findings, and recommendations. Here's a standard structure you can follow:

**1. Title Page**

- **Project Title:** A clear and concise title that accurately reflects the project's subject matter.
- **Author(s) Name(s):** Names of the individuals who authored the report.
- **Affiliation(s):** Organization(s) or institutions the authors are associated with.
- **Date of Submission:** The date the report was submitted.

**Purpose:**

- Clearly identifies the subject matter of the report.
- Provides basic information about the authors and their affiliations.
- Indicates the date of submission, marking the completion of the project.

**Example:**

**Project Title:** Impact of Climate Change on Coastal Ecosystems: A Case Study of [Specific Location]

**Author(s) Name(s):** John Doe, Jane Smith

**Affiliation(s):** University of [University Name], Department of Environmental Science

**Date of Submission:** November 7, 2024

**2. Abstract**

- **Concise Summary:** A brief overview of the entire report, including the project's objectives, methodology, key findings, and conclusions.
- **Keywords:** Relevant keywords to help with indexing and searching.

**Purpose:**

- Provides a concise overview of the entire report.
- Helps readers quickly understand the key points and findings.
- Serves as a summary for those who may not have time to read the entire report.
- Aids in indexing and searching for relevant information.

**Example:**

This study investigates the impact of climate change on coastal ecosystems in [specific location]. Through a combination of field observations, remote sensing data, and statistical analysis, the research explores the effects of sea-level rise, increased storm intensity, and ocean acidification on coastal biodiversity, ecosystem services, and human communities. The findings highlight the vulnerability of coastal ecosystems to climate change and emphasize the need for effective adaptation and mitigation strategies.

**Keywords:** climate change, coastal ecosystems, sea-level rise, storm surge, ocean acidification, biodiversity, ecosystem services, coastal communities, adaptation, mitigation.

**3. Table of Contents**

A list of the main sections and subsections of the report, along with their corresponding page numbers.

**Purpose:**

- Provides a roadmap of the report's structure.

- Helps readers quickly locate specific sections.
- Improves readability and navigation.

**Example:**
**Table of Contents**



**4. List of Figures/Tables**

**Figure/Table Numbers and Titles:** A list of all figures and tables included in the report, with their corresponding page numbers.

**Purpose:**

- Provides a quick reference for figures and tables.
- Helps readers locate specific figures or tables.
- Improves the overall organization of the report.

**Example:**
**List of Figures**



**List of Tables**



**5. Introduction**

Provide context and background information about the project. Clearly state the problem or issue the project aims to address. Specify the specific goals and aims of the project. Define the boundaries and limitations of the project.

**Purpose:**

- Sets the stage for the entire report.
- Provides necessary background information.
- Clearly states the problem or research question.
- Outlines the specific objectives of the study.
- Defines the scope and limitations of the research.

**Example:**

Coastal ecosystems are facing increasing pressure from climate change, particularly sea-level rise, increased storm intensity, and ocean acidification. These factors can lead to significant erosion, habitat loss, and biodiversity decline. This study focuses on the [specific location] coastline, a region known for its diverse marine ecosystems and significant economic and ecological value. The primary objective of this research is to assess the impact of climate change on coastal ecosystems in [specific location] and to identify potential adaptation and mitigation strategies.

**Problem Statement:** Climate change poses a serious threat to the ecological integrity and economic viability of coastal ecosystems in [specific location].

**Research Objectives:**

1. To assess the current state of coastal ecosystems in [specific location].
2. To quantify the rate of sea-level rise and coastal erosion in the study area.
3. To evaluate the impact of climate change on biodiversity and ecosystem services.
4. To identify potential adaptation and mitigation strategies to protect coastal ecosystems.

**Scope:** This study focuses on the [specific coastal area] and will utilize a combination of field surveys, remote sensing data, and historical records to assess the impact of climate change. The analysis will be limited to the period between [start date] and [end date].

**6. Methodology**

Explain the overall research design or approach used. Describe the methods used to collect data, such as surveys, interviews, experiments, or literature reviews. Explain the techniques used to analyze the collected data, such as statistical analysis or qualitative analysis.

**Purpose:**

- Outlines the research design and methodology.
- Explains the data collection methods used.
- Describes the data analysis techniques employed.
- Justifies the chosen methodology.

**Example:**

**Research Design:** A mixed-methods approach, combining quantitative and qualitative methods, will be employed in this study.

**Data Collection Methods:**

- **Field Surveys:** Regular field surveys will be conducted to collect data on coastal erosion, vegetation cover, and benthic communities.
- **Remote Sensing:** High-resolution satellite imagery will be used to monitor changes in coastline morphology, vegetation cover, and water quality.
- **Historical Data:** Historical data on sea-level rise, storm events, and coastal erosion will be collected from government agencies and scientific literature.

**Data Analysis Techniques:**

- **Statistical Analysis:** Statistical techniques, such as regression analysis and trend analysis, will be used to analyze quantitative data.
- **Spatial Analysis:** Geographic Information Systems (GIS) will be used to map and analyze spatial patterns of coastal change.
- **Qualitative Analysis:** Content analysis will be used to analyze qualitative data from interviews and field observations.

By combining these methods, this study aims to provide a comprehensive understanding of the impact of climate change on coastal ecosystems in [specific location].

**7. Results and Findings**

**Purpose:**

- Presents the key findings of the research.
- Visualizes data using tables, charts, and graphs.
- Interprets the results in the context of the research questions.

**Example:**
**Presentation of Results:**

- **Sea-Level Rise:** The analysis of historical tide gauge data and satellite altimetry data revealed a significant increase in sea-level rise rates along the [specific location] coastline, averaging [rate] mm/year over the past [time period].
- **Coastal Erosion:** Field surveys and remote sensing data indicated significant coastal erosion rates, particularly in areas with [specific coastal features]. The highest erosion rates were observed in [specific locations].
- **Impact on Biodiversity:** The loss of coastal habitats, such as mangroves and salt marshes, due to sea-level rise and coastal erosion has led to a decline in biodiversity. Several species, including [specific species], have been identified as vulnerable to climate change impacts.

**Interpretation of Results:**

The observed increase in sea-level rise and coastal erosion rates poses a significant threat to the ecological integrity and economic value of [specific location]. The loss of coastal habitats and biodiversity has implications for ecosystem services, such as coastal protection, fisheries, and tourism. The findings of this study highlight the urgent need for effective adaptation and mitigation strategies to protect coastal ecosystems and communities.

**8. Discussion**

**Purpose:**

- Analyzes the results in depth.
- Compares the findings to existing knowledge and theories.
- Discusses the implications of the findings.
- Acknowledges the limitations of the study.

**Example:**

The results of this study are consistent with previous research on the impact of climate change on coastal ecosystems. However, the magnitude of sea-level rise and coastal erosion rates observed in [specific location] is higher than the global average, suggesting that this region is particularly vulnerable to climate change impacts.

One limitation of this study is the relatively short duration of the data collection period. Long-term monitoring is necessary to fully assess the long-term impacts of climate change on coastal ecosystems. Additionally, future research could explore the socioeconomic impacts of coastal erosion and sea-level rise on local communities.

The findings of this study emphasize the need for proactive measures to protect coastal ecosystems and communities. Potential adaptation strategies include coastal armoring, beach nourishment, and nature-based solutions, such as mangrove restoration. However, it is important to consider the potential trade-offs and long-term effectiveness of these strategies.

**9. Conclusion**

- **Summary of Key Findings:** Summarize the main findings of the project.
- **Achieved Objectives:** Discuss how the project objectives were met.

**10. Recommendations**

- **Practical Recommendations:** Provide specific recommendations based on the findings and conclusions.
- **Future Research Directions:** Suggest potential areas for further research.

**11. References**

- **Citation Style:** Cite all sources used in the report using a consistent citation style (e.g., APA, MLA, Chicago).

**12. Appendix**

- **Supplementary Material:** Include any additional information that supports the main body of the report, such as raw data, detailed calculations, or extended discussions.

Remember to tailor the structure to the specific requirements of your project and the target audience. A well-organized and well-written project report will effectively communicate your findings and recommendations.

**EXAMPLE OF PROJECT REPORT**

**Project Title: Impact of Social Media on Adolescent Mental Health**

**Abstract:**

This study investigates the impact of social media use on the mental health of adolescents. By conducting a comprehensive literature review and analyzing survey data from a sample of [number] adolescents, this research explores the relationship between social media usage, depression, anxiety, and self-esteem. The findings suggest that excessive social media use may contribute to negative mental health outcomes, particularly among adolescents who are already vulnerable to mental health issues.

**Introduction:**

Social media platforms have become an integral part of modern society, especially for adolescents. While these platforms offer numerous benefits, such as social connectivity and information access, they also raise concerns about their potential negative impact on mental health. This study aims to explore the complex relationship between social media use and adolescent mental health.

**Methodology:**

A quantitative research design was employed to collect data from a sample of [number] adolescents aged [age range] years. A self-administered questionnaire was used to gather information on demographics, social media usage patterns, and mental health symptoms. The questionnaire included validated scales to measure depression, anxiety, and self-esteem.

**Results and Discussion:**

The findings of this study indicate a significant correlation between excessive social media use and increased symptoms of depression, anxiety, and decreased self-esteem. Adolescents who spent more time on social media were more likely to report feeling lonely, isolated, and negatively compared to their peers.

**Conclusion:**

This study highlights the potential negative impact of excessive social media use on adolescent mental health. It is crucial for parents, educators, and mental health professionals to be aware of these risks and to promote healthy and balanced social media use. Future research should explore the underlying mechanisms linking social media use to mental health outcomes, as well as develop effective interventions to mitigate these risks.

**Recommendations:**

- Digital Mindfulness: Encourage adolescents to practice digital mindfulness, setting limits on social media use and taking regular breaks.
- Critical Media Literacy: Educate adolescents about the potential biases and misinformation present on social media.
- Positive Online Experiences: Promote positive online interactions and encourage participation in online communities that foster empathy and support.
- Mental Health Support: Provide easy access to mental health resources and support services for adolescents experiencing mental health difficulties.

**References:**

[List of references cited in the report, formatted according to the appropriate style guide, such as APA or MLA]

Note: This is a simplified example. A comprehensive research report would include a more detailed literature review, a rigorous data analysis, and a deeper discussion of the findings.

# TWELVE
# TYPES OF REPORTS

Reports are essential tools for conveying information, analyzing data, and making recommendations. They can vary widely in format, style, and purpose. Here are some common types of reports:

**Informational Reports**

**Progress Reports:** These reports track the advancement of a project or task over time. They outline the work completed, any challenges encountered, and future plans. They are essential for keeping stakeholders informed and ensuring the project stays on schedule and within budget.

**Periodic Reports** :Periodic reports are generated at regular intervals, such as monthly or quarterly. They provide a snapshot of the organization's performance, financial health, or operational activities. These reports are crucial for decision-making, strategic planning, and compliance purposes.

**Investigative Reports** :These reports delve into specific issues or problems to uncover underlying causes and recommend solutions. They are often used to investigate incidents, accidents, or complaints. Investigative reports require a thorough and objective analysis of the situation.

**Compliance Reports** : Compliance reports demonstrate an organization's adherence to specific regulations, industry standards, or internal policies. These reports are essential for maintaining legal and ethical standards and avoiding penalties or legal actions.

**Feasibility Reports** : Feasibility reports assess the viability of a proposed project or idea. They evaluate factors such as technical feasibility, economic feasibility, and legal feasibility. These reports help organizations make informed decisions about whether to proceed with a project or not.

**Analytical Reports**

**Financial Reports** : Provide a clear and accurate picture of an organization's financial health. Income statements, balance sheets, cash flow statements, and financial ratios.

**Market Research Reports** : Gather and analyze information about a market to identify opportunities and challenges. Market size, target audience segmentation, competitive analysis, consumer behavior analysis, and market trends.

**Technical Reports** : Document technical information, such as research findings, engineering designs, or scientific discoveries. Detailed methodology, data analysis, results, conclusions, and recommendations.

**Business Reports** : Analyze business performance and provide insights to support decision-making. Performance metrics, SWOT analysis, financial analysis, market analysis, and strategic recommendations.

**Proposal Reports**

**Grant Proposals:** Detail the project's objectives, methodology, budget, and expected outcomes. Persuade potential funders to allocate resources to the project.

**Business Proposals:** Outline a business idea or plan, including market analysis, financial projections, and a detailed implementation strategy. Convince investors or clients of the project's viability and potential return on investment.

**Other Types**

**Minutes of Meetings:** Record key decisions, action items, and discussions from meetings. Serve as a reference document for future meetings and decision-making.

**Incident Reports:** Document the details of accidents or incidents, including the date, time, location, and involved parties. Analyze the root causes of incidents and recommend preventive measures.

**Audit Reports:** Assess the financial health, operational efficiency, and compliance of an organization. Identify areas for improvement and provide recommendations for corrective actions.

## TYPES OF PROJECT REPORT

### Academic Project Reports

- These reports are typically submitted as part of a course curriculum. They focus on theoretical knowledge application, research methodology, and analysis.

- Characteristics: Formal structure, emphasis on research and analysis, use of academic referencing, evaluation of theoretical frameworks.

**Examples:** Undergraduate and postgraduate dissertations, lab reports, case studies, literature reviews.

**Industry Project Reports**

Prepared for a professional setting, these reports focus on practical applications and business outcomes.

- Characteristics: Clear and concise language, emphasis on results and recommendations, use of industry-specific metrics, alignment with business objectives.

**Examples:** Feasibility studies, market analysis reports, project proposals, project closure reports.

**Research Project Reports**

**These reports detail original research conducted to contribute to existing knowledge.**

- Characteristics: Rigorous methodology, detailed data analysis, contribution to the field, adherence to research ethics.

**Examples:** Scientific research papers, thesis, grant proposals.

**WRITING STYLE AND TONE**

**Formal and Objective Language**

- Avoid colloquialisms, contractions, and personal pronouns (I, we, you).
- Maintain a neutral and impersonal tone.
- Use precise and specific language to convey information accurately.
- Example: Instead of "The thing is really cool," write "The experiment yielded promising results."

**Clear and Concise Writing**

- Use direct and simple sentence structure.
- Avoid unnecessary jargon and complex sentence constructions.
- Get to the point quickly.
- Prioritize clarity over complexity.

**Example:** Instead of "In the event that the data is inconclusive, further research may be warranted," write "If the data is inconclusive, additional research is needed."

**Appropriate Use of Technical Terms**

- Define technical terms when first used.
- Use consistent terminology throughout the report.
- Avoid overuse of jargon that might confuse the reader.
- Consider your audience's level of expertise.
- Example: If using a term like "correlation coefficient," explain its meaning clearly.

**Consistent Formatting**

- Adhere to a specific style guide (APA, MLA, Chicago, etc.).
- Maintain consistent font, font size, and line spacing.
- Use headings and subheadings effectively to organize the content.
- Ensure consistent formatting for tables, figures, and citations.
- Example: Use the same font and font size for all headings throughout the report.

## TOOLS FOR REPORT WRITING

**Word Processing Software**

Core tool for report creation and formatting.

**Examples:** Microsoft Word, Google Docs, LibreOffice Writer.

- **Key features:**
    - Text formatting (fonts, styles, spacing)
    - Page layout and design
    - Inserting images, tables, and charts
    - Spell and grammar checking
    - Collaboration features (for some software)

**Citation Management Tools**

- Organize and format bibliographic information.
- Generate citations and reference lists automatically.

**Examples:** Zotero, Mendeley, EndNote.

- **Key features:**
  - Import citations from various sources (databases, PDFs)
  - Create bibliographies in different citation styles (APA, MLA, Chicago)
  - Organize research materials (notes, PDFs, images)

**Presentation Software**

- Create visual aids to accompany the report.
- **Examples:** Microsoft PowerPoint, Google Slides, Apple Keynote.
- **Key features:**
  - Design templates and themes
  - Adding text, images, charts, and videos
  - Animation and transitions
  - Presenter notes

  - Slide show mode

# THIRTEEN

# PURPOSE OF REPORT WRITING

Reports serve as a vital tool for communication, decision-making, and knowledge sharing. Their primary purpose is to:

1. **Inform:**
    - **Conveying Information:** Clearly and concisely present information to a specific audience.
    - **Explaining Complex Topics:** Breaking down complex ideas into understandable terms.
    - **Providing Updates:** Sharing progress on projects or initiatives.
2. **Analyze:**
    - **Evaluating Data:** Analyzing data to identify trends, patterns, and insights.
    - **Identifying Problems:** Pinpointing issues or challenges that need to be addressed.
    - **Assessing Performance:** Evaluating the performance of individuals, teams, or organizations.
3. **Persuade:**
    - **Influencing Decisions:** Convincing readers to take a specific course of action.

  - **Securing Funding:** Persuading potential funders to support a project or initiative.
  - **Promoting Ideas:** Advocating for new ideas or approaches.

4. **Document:**

  - **Creating a Record:** Preserving information for future reference.
  - **Complying with Regulations:** Adhering to legal and regulatory requirements.
  - **Sharing Knowledge:** Transferring knowledge and best practices within an organization.

These purposes, reports contribute to informed decision-making, problem-solving, and overall organizational success.

# FOURTEEN
# INTENDED AUDIENCE

Your target audience is the specific group of people you aim to reach with your project report. They are the individuals most likely to be interested in, benefit from, or be affected by the information you present. It's essential to define your target audience clearly to tailor your report effectively.

**Intended audience:**

- Volunteers
- Supporters
- New Recruits
- Media
- Generic/Targeted Public
- Alies/Parnters

The intended audience of a report refers to the specific group of people for whom the report is written. Understanding your audience is crucial for tailoring the content, style, and tone of your report to their needs and interests.

**Tips to determine your intended audience**

- Segment Your Audience
- Do research on the market
- Look at your Competitions
- Look at industry trends
- Take with your audience
- Interpret data

**Key Considerations for Identifying Your Intended Audience:**

- Consider factors like age, gender, education level, and occupation.
- Assess the audience's prior knowledge of the subject matter.
- Determine what specific aspects of the topic interest your audience.
- Understand what your audience hopes to gain from the report.

**Why Identifying Your Intended Audience is Important:**

- Tailoring your language and style to your audience's level of understanding enhances comprehension.
- By knowing your audience's needs and concerns, you can craft a more persuasive message.
- A well-targeted report is more likely to achieve its intended purpose, whether it's informing, persuading, or motivating.

**General Example:**

**Young Adults:** Many books target young adults specifically, creating novels that deal with coming-of-age issues.

**Students:** The intended audience of study websites (like Helpful Professor) is students. And many advertisers like to target students, too!

**Example:**

Let's say you're writing a report on the environmental impact of a new technology. Your intended audience could be:

- Technical Experts: In this case, you would focus on the technical details, using specialized jargon and citing relevant research.
- Policymakers: For policymakers, you would emphasize the potential policy implications and regulatory framework.
- General Public: For a general audience, you would simplify the technical language and focus on the broader impact of the technology.

By understanding your intended audience, you can create a report that is clear, concise, and effective.

# FIFTEEN
# PLAGIARISM

Plagiarism is the act of presenting someone else's work or ideas as your own without giving proper credit. This includes copying and pasting text, paraphrasing without citation, or using another person's work without acknowledging the source.

**Types of Plagiarism**

**1. Direct Plagiarism**

- Copying text verbatim from a source without proper attribution.
- Example: Taking a sentence or paragraph from a book, article, or website and inserting it directly into your own work without using quotation marks or citing the source.

**2. Paraphrasing Plagiarism**

- Restating someone else's ideas in your own words without proper citation.
- Example: Changing a few words or sentence structure, but keeping the original meaning and structure of the source material.

**3. Self-Plagiarism**

- Reusing your own previously published work without proper citation.
- Submitting the same paper or parts of a paper to multiple courses or publications without acknowledging the prior use.

**4. Mosaic Plagiarism**

- Combining ideas or phrases from multiple sources without proper citation.
- Example: Taking phrases or sentences from different sources and stringing them together to form a new piece of text without proper attribution.

It's important to note that even unintentional plagiarism can have serious consequences. To avoid plagiarism, always cite your sources correctly and use quotation marks for direct quotes. If you're unsure about how to cite something, consult your instructor or a citation style guide.

**How to Avoid Plagiarism:**

**To ensure academic integrity and avoid plagiarism, follow these guidelines:**

**1. Cite Your Sources**

- Employ a consistent citation style (e.g., APA, MLA, Chicago) to accurately credit the original authors.
- Provide complete citation details, including author names, publication titles, dates, and page numbers.

**2. Paraphrase Correctly**

- Thoroughly comprehend the original text.
- Rewrite the information using your own vocabulary and sentence structure.
- Even when paraphrasing, cite the original source to acknowledge the original ideas.

**3. Quote Accurately**

- Enclose the exact words from the source in quotation marks.
- Introduce the quote and explain its relevance to your work.
- Cite the source of the quote using the appropriate citation style.

**4. Use Plagiarism Checking Tools**

- Utilize tools like Turnitin to scan your work for similarities to existing sources.

- Use the tool's feedback to identify and correct any instances of plagiarism.

**5. Understand Fair Use**

- Be aware of copyright laws and understand the limitations on using copyrighted material.
- Familiarize yourself with fair use guidelines, which allow limited use of copyrighted material for specific purposes.
- When in doubt, obtain permission from the copyright holder to use the material.

These guidelines, you can ensure the integrity of your work and avoid the serious consequences of plagiarism.

**Consequences of Plagiarism:**

KJK Plagiarism can have severe consequences for both students and professionals. Here are some of the potential consequences:

**Academic Penalties**

- Plagiarized assignments can result in failing grades for the course or even the entire academic year.
- Students may be placed on academic probation, which can restrict their academic activities and eligibility for certain programs.
- In severe cases of plagiarism, students may be expelled from their educational institution.

**Professional Consequences**

- Plagiarism can damage your reputation and credibility as a researcher or professional.
- If discovered, plagiarism can lead to job loss or termination of contracts.
- In some cases, plagiarism may result in legal action, including lawsuits and fines.

**Ethical Implications**

- Plagiarism undermines your academic and professional integrity.

- It violates the trust placed in you by your instructors, colleagues, and employers.
- Plagiarism gives you an unfair advantage over other students or professionals who do their own work.

To avoid these consequences, it's essential to always cite your sources properly and to understand the principles of academic integrity. The concept of plagiarism and following proper citation practices, you can avoid academic dishonesty and maintain your academic integrity.

**Example of Plagiarism:**

**Original Text:**

"Climate change is a global threat that requires urgent action. Rising temperatures, extreme weather events, and sea-level rise are already impacting communities worldwide. To mitigate these effects, it is essential to reduce greenhouse gas emissions and transition to renewable energy sources."

**Plagiarized Text (Direct Plagiarism):**

Climate change is a global threat that requires urgent action. Rising temperatures, extreme weather events, and sea-level rise are already impacting communities worldwide. To mitigate these effects, it is essential to reduce greenhouse gas emissions and transition to renewable energy sources.

**Plagiarized Text (Paraphrasing Plagiarism):**

The world is facing a climate crisis, marked by increasing temperatures, severe weather patterns, and rising sea levels. To combat this issue, it's imperative to decrease greenhouse gas emissions and adopt renewable energy solutions.

# SIXTEEN

# REPORT WRITING IN STEM FIELDS

A project report is a comprehensive document that outlines the details, progress, and outcomes of a specific project. It serves as a formal record of the project's lifecycle, from initiation to completion. This document provides stakeholders with a clear understanding of the project's purpose, scope, and deliverables.

**What is STEM in project report writing ?**

**STEM** stands for **Science, Technology, Engineering, and Mathematics.**

In the context of project report writing, STEM refers to projects that involve these four disciplines. These projects often require:

- **Scientific Inquiry**: Conducting experiments, collecting data, and analyzing results.
- **Technological Application**: Using technology tools and software to solve problems.
- **Engineering Design:** Designing and building solutions to real-world problems.
- **Mathematical Modeling:** Using mathematical concepts to model and analyze complex systems.

STEM project reports typically include detailed descriptions of the project's goals, methodology, results, and conclusions. They often involve presenting data in various formats, such as graphs, charts, and tables.

**PURPOSE OF A STEM REPORT**

The purpose of a STEM report is to effectively communicate research findings, methodologies, and conclusions to a specific audience. It serves as a formal record of a project or experiment, providing a clear and comprehensive overview of the work undertaken.

More specifically, a STEM report aims to:

- **Inform:** Present factual information about the research, including data, results, and analysis.
- **Educate:** Explain complex concepts and methodologies in a clear and understandable manner.
- **Persuade:** Convince the reader of the validity and significance of the research findings.
- **Document:** Create a permanent record of the project for future reference and evaluation.
- **Contribute:** Advance knowledge in the field by sharing new discoveries and insights.

**Importance of Effective Report Writing in STEM**

Effective report writing in STEM is crucial for several reasons:

- **Communication of Findings:** It enables researchers and scientists to clearly and accurately convey their research findings to a wide audience, including peers, policymakers, and the public.
- **Knowledge Dissemination:** It contributes to the advancement of knowledge in the field by sharing research results and methodologies.
- **Collaboration:** It facilitates collaboration among researchers by providing a common platform for sharing information and ideas.
- **Evaluation and Assessment:** It serves as a basis for evaluating the project's success and identifying areas for improvement.
- **Funding Acquisition:** Well-written reports are essential for securing funding for future research projects.

**Key Characteristics of a Good STEM Report**

**Conciseness:**

- A good STEM report presents information in a clear and direct manner, avoiding unnecessary details.

- It focuses on the most important findings and conclusions, without sacrificing essential information.

**Clarity:**

- The report is written in clear and simple language, avoiding jargon and technical terms that may confuse the reader.
- The structure of the report is logical, with information presented in a clear and organized manner.

**Objectivity:**

- A STEM report should present information in an unbiased and impartial manner.
- Avoid personal opinions and subjective interpretations.

**Accuracy:**

- The information presented in the report must be correct and verifiable.
- Use accurate data, measurements, and calculations.

**Importance of Knowing the Target Audience**

Understanding your target audience is paramount in crafting an effective STEM report. It enables you to tailor the content, language, and level of detail to meet the specific needs and expectations of your readers. By identifying your audience, you can ensure that the report is clear, relevant, and impactful.

**Tailoring the Report to Different Readers**

The content and style of a STEM report can vary significantly depending on the target audience. Three primary audiences and how to tailor the report accordingly:

- Academics
- Industry Professionals
- Policymakers

**Writing Style and Tone in STEM Reports**

**Importance of Clear and Concise Writing**

- In STEM, clarity and conciseness are paramount. Readers, often with limited time, need to grasp information quickly.
- **Directness:** Avoid unnecessary words and phrases.
- **Simplicity:** Use plain language and straightforward sentence structure.
- **Focus:** Prioritize essential information.

**Use of Active Voice**

- Active voice makes writing more direct and engaging. It clearly conveys who is performing an action.
- **Example:**
    - Passive: The experiment was conducted by the researchers.
    - Active: The researchers conducted the experiment.

**Avoiding Jargon and Technical Terms**

While some technical terms are inevitable, overuse can hinder understanding.

- Explain technical terms when first used.
- Use jargon judiciously, considering your audience.
- Prioritize understanding over impressing with complex language.

**Maintaining Objectivity**

STEM writing demands objectivity. Avoid personal opinions and biases.

- Base conclusions on data and observations.
- Present information without emotional language.
- Be transparent about research constraints.

**Editing and Proofreading STEM Writing**

Editing is a critical step in refining a STEM report. It involves assessing the overall structure, content, and clarity of the document. Careful editing ensures that:

- Ideas are well-organized and logically presented.
- Information is accurate and relevant.
- Writing is concise and engaging.

- The report adheres to the required style guide (APA, MLA, Chicago, etc.).

**Peer Review as a Tool for Improvement**

Peer review is invaluable for enhancing the quality of STEM writing. By sharing your work with colleagues, you can:

- Gain different perspectives on your research.
- Identify areas for improvement in clarity and coherence.
- Receive feedback on the overall effectiveness of the report.
- Improve your writing skills by learning from others' feedback.

**EXAMPLE**

**STEM Project Report: Building a Solar-Powered Water Purifier**

**Introduction**

This report details the design, construction, and testing of a solar-powered water purifier. The project aims to provide clean drinking water in areas with limited access to clean water sources. By combining solar energy with water purification techniques, this device offers a sustainable and efficient solution.

**Design and Methodology**

**Design:**

- **Solar Panel:** A photovoltaic panel to convert sunlight into electrical energy.
- **Water Pump:** A submersible pump powered by the solar panel to draw water from a source.
- **Water Filtration System:** A multi-stage filtration system consisting of a coarse filter, activated carbon filter, and UV sterilizer.
- **Storage Tank:** A water storage tank to store purified water.

**Methodology:**

1. **Research:** Extensive research was conducted on solar energy, water purification techniques, and relevant materials.
2. **Design and Prototyping:** A 3D model of the purifier was created using [software name]. The physical prototype was constructed using [materials used].

3. **Testing and Optimization:** The purifier was tested under various conditions, including different water sources and solar irradiance levels. Adjustments were made to optimize performance.

**Results and Discussion**

The solar-powered water purifier demonstrated effective performance in purifying water from various sources. The UV sterilization process effectively eliminated bacteria and viruses, ensuring the safety of the purified water. The solar panel provided sufficient power to operate the pump and filtration system during daylight hours.

However, the system's performance was affected by cloudy weather conditions and low solar irradiance. Future improvements could include incorporating a battery storage system to provide power during nighttime or cloudy days.

**Conclusion**

The successful design and implementation of this solar-powered water purifier highlight the potential of combining technology and sustainable practices to address global water challenges. By harnessing solar energy, this device offers a promising solution for providing clean drinking water in remote and resource-constrained areas.

**Future Work**

- Explore alternative water purification techniques, such as reverse osmosis.
- Develop a more efficient and compact design.
- Integrate a battery storage system to ensure continuous operation.
- Conduct field testing in various environmental conditions.

**References**

[List of references used in the report]

**Note:** This is a simplified example of a STEM project report. Actual reports may include more detailed information, such as detailed calculations, circuit diagrams, data analysis, and specific experimental procedures.

# SEVENTEEN
# EXPERIMENT

An experiment is a controlled investigation or test designed to gather data and answer a specific question. It involves manipulating one or more variables to observe their effect on another variable.

**Key elements of an experiment include:**

**Independent variable:** The factor that is changed or manipulated by the experimenter.

**Dependent variable:** The factor that is measured or observed and is expected to change in response to the independent variable.

**Control group:** A group that remains constant and unchanged, providing a baseline for comparison.

**Experimental group**: The group exposed to the independent variable.

**Importance of Experimentation in STEM**

Experimentation is the cornerstone of scientific inquiry. It plays a crucial role in:

- Experiments allow scientists to explore the natural world, ask questions, and seek answers through systematic observation and testing.
- By conducting experiments, scientists can test the validity of existing theories or generate new hypotheses to explain observed phenomena.
- Experimentation is essential for discovering new information, creating innovative solutions, and advancing our understanding of the world.

**Key Components of an Experiment**

**Independent Variable**

- The factor that the experimenter manipulates or changes in the experiment.
- It's the variable that is suspected to cause a change in the dependent variable.
- **Example:** In an experiment testing the effect of fertilizer on plant growth, the amount of fertilizer applied would be the independent variable.

**Dependent Variable**

- The factor that is measured or observed in an experiment.
- It's the variable that is expected to change in response to the changes in the independent variable.
- **Example:** In the fertilizer experiment, the height of the plants would be the dependent variable.

**Control Group**

- A group of subjects in an experiment that does not receive the experimental treatment.
- It serves as a baseline for comparison. By keeping all factors constant except for the independent variable, the control group helps isolate the effect of the independent variable on the dependent variable.
- **Example:** In the fertilizer experiment, a group of plants that receive no fertilizer would be the control group.

**Experimental Group**

- A group of subjects in an experiment that receives the experimental treatment.
- This group is exposed to the manipulation of the independent variable, allowing us to observe its effect on the dependent variable.
- **Example:** In the fertilizer experiment, the group of plants that receive different amounts of fertilizer would be the experimental groups.

**Why are these components important?**

- **Independent and Dependent Variables:** They form the core of the experiment, defining the relationship being investigated.
- **Control and Experimental Groups:** They help establish cause-and-effect relationships by isolating the effect of the independent variable. The control group provides a "normal" state for comparison, while the experimental group shows the effect of the treatment.

**Importance of a Well-Designed Experiment**

A well-designed experiment is crucial for generating reliable and valid scientific knowledge. It ensures that the conclusions drawn from the research are accurate and can be trusted.

**Reliability**

Reliability refers to the consistency of a measurement. In the context of experiments, it means that if the experiment were repeated under the same conditions, the results would be similar.

**Factors affecting reliability:**

- Ensuring that procedures are consistent across all participants and trials.
- Reducing measurement error and experimental error.
- Having a large enough sample size to increase the precision of the results.
- Using accurate and precise instruments to collect data.

**Validity**

Validity refers to the accuracy of a measurement. In experiments, it means that the experiment measures what it is intended to measure.

**Types of validity:**

- **Internal validity:** This refers to the extent to which the independent variable truly causes the observed changes in the dependent variable. It is influenced by factors such as control groups, random assignment, and the minimization of confounding variables.
- **External validity:** This refers to the extent to which the results of the experiment can be generalized to other populations or settings. It is influenced by factors such as sample size, representativeness of the sample, and the ecological validity of the experimental conditions.

**Why are reliability and validity important?**

- Reliable and valid experiments enhance the credibility of the research findings.
- **Generalizability:** Valid experiments allow for broader generalizations of the results.
- **Reproducibility:** Reliable experiments can be replicated by other researchers to verify the findings.
- **Informed decision-making:** Reliable and valid research provides a solid foundation for evidence-based decision-making.

By prioritizing reliability and validity in experimental design, researchers can contribute to the advancement of scientific knowledge and improve the quality of research.

**Factors that contribute to a well-designed experiment:**

- **Control of variables:** Minimizing the influence of extraneous variables that could affect the results.
- **Randomization:** Assigning participants or subjects to experimental and control groups randomly to reduce bias.
- **Replication:** Repeating the experiment multiple times to increase confidence in the results.
- **Appropriate sample size:** Using a sufficient number of participants or subjects to ensure statistical power.

**Interpretation of Results in Relation to Research Question**

**Relate findings to research question:** Clearly explain how your results answer or contribute to answering the research question.

**Support or refute hypothesis:** Discuss whether your results support or contradict your original hypothesis.

**Explain unexpected findings:** If your results differ from expectations, provide potential explanations.

**Limitations of the Experiment**

- Be transparent about the shortcomings of your study.
- Explain how these limitations might affect the interpretation of results.
- Propose ways to address these limitations in future research.

**Implications of the Findings**

- Explain how your findings contribute to understanding underlying theories.
- Discuss potential real-world applications of your results.
- Propose new research questions based on your findings.

# EIGHTEEN
# STATISTICAL ANALYSIS

Statistical analysis is the systematic process of collecting, organizing, analyzing, interpreting, and presenting data. It involves applying statistical methods to extract meaningful information from raw data and draw valid conclusions. This process helps in understanding patterns, trends, and relationships within the data.

**Steps in Statistical Analysis**

Here's a step-by-step guide to conducting statistical analysis:

1. **Define the Research Question:**
    - Clearly articulate the problem or question you want to answer.
    - Specify the population and variables of interest.
2. **Data Collection:**
    - **Design the Study:** Determine the appropriate research design (e.g., experimental, observational, survey).
    - **Collect Data:** Gather relevant data using methods like surveys, experiments, or existing datasets.
    - **Ensure Data Quality:** Check for accuracy, completeness, and consistency.
3. **Data Cleaning and Preparation:**
    - **Clean the Data:** Identify and correct errors, inconsistencies, and missing values.

- **Organize the Data:** Structure the data into a suitable format for analysis (e.g., spreadsheet, database).
- **Transform the Data:** If necessary, transform the data (e.g., log transformations, normalization).

1. **Exploratory Data Analysis (EDA):**

    - **Summarize Data:** Calculate descriptive statistics (mean, median, mode, standard deviation, etc.).
    - **Visualize Data:** Create visualizations (histograms, box plots, scatter plots) to understand patterns.
    - **Identify Outliers:** Detect and handle outliers or anomalies.

2. **Hypothesis Testing:**

    - **Formulate Hypotheses:** State the null and alternative hypotheses.
    - **Choose the Appropriate Test:** Select the statistical test based on the research question and data type (e.g., t-test, ANOVA, chi-square test).
    - **Conduct the Test:** Calculate the test statistic and p-value.
    - **Make a Decision:** Compare the p-value to the significance level (e.g., 0.05) to reject or fail to reject the null hypothesis.

3. **Inferential Statistics:**

    - **Confidence Intervals:** Estimate population parameters with a certain level of confidence.
    - **Regression Analysis:** Model the relationship between variables.
    - **Correlation Analysis:** Measure the strength and direction of relationships.

4. **Interpretation and Conclusion:**

    - **Interpret Results:** Explain the findings in plain language.
    - **Draw Conclusions:** Answer the research question based on the statistical analysis.
    - **Consider Limitations:** Acknowledge the limitations of the study.

**Tools for Statistical Analysis:**

- **Statistical Software:**
    - SPSS
    - SAS
    - R
    - Python (with libraries like NumPy, Pandas, SciPy, and Statsmodels)
- **Spreadsheet Software:**
    - Microsoft Excel (for basic statistical functions)

**Key Roles of Statistical Analysis in Project Reports**

1. **Data Summarization:**
    - **Descriptive Statistics:**
        - Central tendency measures (mean, median, mode)
        - Dispersion measures (range, variance, standard deviation)
        - Frequency distributions and histograms
    - These statistics provide a concise overview of the data, highlighting key characteristics.
2. **Data Visualization:**
    - **Graphs and Charts:**
        - Bar charts, line graphs, scatter plots, pie charts
        - Visualizing data helps identify patterns, trends, and anomalies more easily.
3. **Hypothesis Testing:**
    - **Inferential Statistics:**
        - t-tests, ANOVA, chi-square tests

  - These tests allow researchers to draw inferences about a population based on sample data.
  - They help determine the statistical significance of observed differences or relationships.

4. **Correlation Analysis:**

   - **Measuring Relationships:**

     - Pearson correlation coefficient, Spearman's rank correlation coefficient
     - These measures assess the strength and direction of the relationship between two variables.

5. **Regression Analysis:**

   - **Predicting Outcomes:**

     - Linear regression, multiple regression
     - These techniques help predict the value of a dependent variable based on the values of independent variables.

6. **Data Mining and Machine Learning:**

   - **Discovering Patterns:**

     - Clustering, classification, regression
     - These advanced techniques can uncover hidden patterns and insights from large datasets.

**Importance of Statistical Analysis in Project Reports**

- Statistical analysis provides an objective way to analyze data, reducing bias.
- It allows for precise quantification of findings.
- Statistical methods enable researchers to draw conclusions about the broader population.

- Statistical analysis supports informed decision-making by providing evidence-based insights.
- Well-conducted statistical analysis enhances the credibility of research findings.

**Tips for Effective Statistical Analysis in Project Reports**

- Formulate clear and specific research questions to guide the analysis.
- Choose statistical methods that are suitable for the research design and data type.
- Ensure data accuracy and completeness to avoid biased results.
- Interpret statistical results correctly and avoid overinterpretation.
- Use clear and effective visualizations to communicate findings.
- Acknowledge the limitations of the analysis and the assumptions made.
- Adhere to ethical guidelines for data collection and analysis.

By effectively utilizing statistical analysis, researchers can produce high-quality project reports that contribute to knowledge and inform decision-making.

# NINETEEN
# FRAMING A TITLE

A well-crafted title is the first impression of your project report. It should be concise, informative, and engaging. Here are some key considerations for framing an effective title:

**Key Considerations for a Good Title:**

1. **Clarity and Conciseness:**
    - Clearly state the main topic of your project.
    - Use simple language that is understandable to a broad audience.
    - Aim for a title that is no more than 15 words.
2. **Informativeness:**
    - Include the primary variables or concepts investigated.
    - Indicate the breadth and depth of your research.
    - Briefly mention the research approach (e.g., experimental, survey, case study).
3. **Engaging:**
    - Start with action verbs to grab the reader's attention.
    - Stimulate curiosity and intrigue.
    - Use creative language to make your title memorable.

**4. Relevance to the Content:**

- Reflect the main theme: Ensure the title accurately represents the project's focus.
- Avoid misleading statements: Don't make claims that the content doesn't support.
- Consider the target audience: Tailor the title to the interests and knowledge level of your readers.

**5. Formatting and Style:**

- Capitalization: Use proper capitalization conventions (e.g., title case for words at the beginning of phrases).
- Punctuation: Avoid unnecessary punctuation, such as commas or colons.
- Formatting: Follow any specific guidelines or templates provided by your institution or organization.

**6. Brainstorming Techniques:**

- Keyword analysis: Identify the most important terms related to your project.
- Question-and-answer: Ask yourself questions about the topic and try to answer them in a concise way.
- Mind mapping: Visually organize your thoughts and ideas to create a comprehensive overview.

**COMMON TITLE STRUCTURES:**

**1. Declarative Title**

Directly states the main finding or conclusion.

**Example:** "The Impact of Social Media on Adolescent Mental Health"

**Other examples:**

- "Climate Change and Rising Sea Levels: A Threat to Coastal Communities"
- "The Efficacy of Online Learning in Higher Education"
- "The Influence of Mindfulness Meditation on Stress Reduction"

**2. Question-Based Title**

Poses a question that the research aims to answer.

**Example:** "Can Mindfulness Meditation Improve Academic Performance?"

**Other examples:**

- "Does Early Childhood Education Impact Future Academic Success?"
- "How Does Social Media Affect Body Image and Self-Esteem?"
- "What is the Impact of Artificial Intelligence on Job Market Trends?"

**3. Comparative Title**

Compares two or more variables or groups.

**Example:** "A Comparative Analysis of Traditional and Online Learning"

**Other examples:**

- "Comparing the Effectiveness of Different Teaching Methods"
- "A Comparative Study of Urban and Rural Education Systems"
- "A Comparative Analysis of Organic and Conventional Farming Practices"

**4. How-To Title**

Provides a solution or recommendation.

**Example:** "How to Enhance Employee Engagement Through Gamification"

**Other examples:**

- "A Step-by-Step Guide to Effective Time Management"
- "Strategies for Improving Student Motivation in the Classroom"
- "A Practical Guide to Reducing Workplace Stress"

**TIPS FOR CRAFTING A STRONG TITLE:**

- Brainstorm: Generate multiple ideas and select the most compelling one.
- Consult with Others: Get feedback from peers, mentors, or supervisors.
- Revise and Edit: Refine your title until it is clear, concise, and impactful.
- Consider Your Audience: Tailor the title to the specific audience you are targeting.
- Use Keywords: Incorporate relevant keywords to improve search engine visibility.

**Framing a Title to Attract Reader Attention**

A captivating title is crucial for drawing readers into your work. It should be informative, intriguing, and memorable. Here are five examples that demonstrate effective techniques for crafting attention-grabbing titles:

**1. Using Strong Verbs and Keywords:**

- Example: "Unleashing the Power of AI: Revolutionizing Customer Service"
- Explanation: The strong verb "unleashing" creates a sense of excitement and anticipation. The keyword "AI" immediately piques interest, especially for readers interested in technology.

**2. Asking a Provocative Question:**

- Example: "Is Your Business Ready for the Future of Work?"
- Explanation: A question poses a challenge or curiosity, encouraging readers to seek answers. This title suggests that the content may offer valuable insights for business professionals.

**3. Creating a Sense of Urgency or Scarcity:**

- Example: "Limited Time Offer: Discover the Secrets to Effective Time Management"
- Explanation: The phrase "Limited Time Offer" creates a sense of urgency, making readers feel like they might miss out if they don't act quickly.

**4. Using a Play on Words or Alliteration:**

- Example: "Beyond the Buzz: A Deep Dive into Digital Marketing Trends"
- Explanation: A play on words or alliteration makes the title more memorable and engaging. This title also hints at the content's depth and analysis.

**5. Highlighting a Unique Benefit or Solution:**

- Example: "Boost Your Productivity by 20% with These Proven Strategies"
- Explanation: This title clearly states a tangible benefit that readers can expect to gain from the content. It immediately grabs attention by offering a specific solution to a common problem.

**EXAMPLE:**
**Topic: The impact of climate change on coastal ecosystems**
**Possible Titles:**

- **Declarative:** Climate Change Erodes Coastal Ecosystems
- **Question-Based:** How Does Climate Change Threaten Coastal Ecosystems?
- **Comparative:** Coastal Ecosystems: A Comparative Analysis of Natural and Human-Induced Threats
- **How-To:** Mitigating Climate Change Impacts on Coastal Ecosystems

These guidelines and considering the specific nature of your project, you can create a compelling and informative title that will attract readers and effectively communicate the essence of your research.

# TWENTY

# CONTENT

n the digital age, content is the lifeblood of the project . It encompasses a wide range of formats, including text, images, videos, and audio. Essentially, content is any information or experience that is shared online.

**Why is Content Important?**

Content serves multiple purposes:

**Informs:** Provides users with valuable information and knowledge.

- Educational Content: Blog posts, articles, and tutorials that teach users new skills or concepts.
- How-To Guides: Step-by-step instructions on how to complete a task or solve a problem.
- Product Information: Detailed descriptions of products or services.
- Industry News and Trends: Updates on the latest developments in a specific field.

**Engages:** Captures the attention of the audience and sparks interest.

- Storytelling: Using narratives to connect with the audience on an emotional level.
- Visual Appeal: Using images, videos, and infographics to make content visually appealing.
- Interactive Content: Quizzes, polls, and calculators that encourage user participation.
- Humor and Wit: Using humor to make content more enjoyable and memorable.

**Persuades:** Influences the audience's opinions or behaviors.

- Call to Action: Encouraging users to take a specific action, such as making a purchase or signing up for a newsletter.
- Social Proof: Using testimonials and reviews to build trust and credibility.
- Emotional Appeal: Using emotions to persuade the audience (e.g., fear, guilt, hope).
- Logical Appeal: Using facts and evidence to support your argument.

**Entertains:** Provides enjoyment and relaxation.

- Humor and Satire: Using humor to make content entertaining.
- Games and Puzzles: Interactive content that challenges the user.
- Pop Culture References: Using references to popular culture to connect with the audience.
- Personal Stories: Sharing personal experiences to build empathy and connection.

By understanding these roles, you can create content that is not only informative but also engaging, persuasive, and enjoyable. This will help you build a loyal audience and achieve your marketing goals.

**Types of Content**

- Blog Posts: Written articles that provide information, tips, or stories.
- Articles: In-depth pieces of writing on specific topics.
- Videos: Visual content that can explain, demonstrate, or entertain.
- Infographics: Visual representations of information.
- Social Media Posts: Short-form content for platforms like Twitter, Instagram, and Facebook.
- Email Newsletters: Regular emails with curated content.
- Webinars and Podcasts: Online seminars and audio broadcasts.
- Whitepapers and eBooks: Comprehensive guides on specific topics.

**The Role of Content in project Report writing**

Content is the backbone of a project report. It conveys information, analysis, and insights, enabling effective communication and decision-making. Here's a breakdown of its crucial role:

**1. Clarity and Conciseness:**

- Well-structured and concise content ensures that the message is easily understood.
- Use clear and direct language, avoiding jargon and technical terms.

**2. Informative and Engaging:**

- Present only the most relevant information to the project's objectives.
- Use a clear and concise writing style that keeps the reader interested.
- Employ visuals like charts, graphs, and diagrams to enhance understanding.

**3. Accurate and Reliable:**

- Ensure the accuracy and reliability of all data and information presented.
- Verify all sources and references to maintain credibility.

**4. Objective Analysis:**

- Present information objectively, avoiding personal biases.
- Analyze data critically and draw meaningful conclusions.

**5. Effective Storytelling:**

- Organize the content in a logical and engaging narrative.
- Use storytelling techniques to make the report more interesting and memorable.

**6. Adherence to Formatting Guidelines:**

- Use a consistent format throughout the report (font, font size, line spacing, margins).
- Use headings, subheadings, and bullet points to improve readability.

## STEPS TO DEVELOP CONTENT IN PROJECT REPORT WRITING

Here are the key steps to develop effective content for your project report:

**1. Understand Your Audience and Purpose:**

- Identify your target audience: Who will be reading your report?
- Determine the purpose: What is the goal of your report? Is it to inform, persuade, or explain?

2. Gather Relevant Information:

- Collect data: Gather all necessary data, such as research findings, statistics, and case studies.
- Organize your information: Structure your information in a logical and easy-to-follow manner.

**3. Develop a Clear Structure:**

- Create an outline: Outline the main sections of your report, including the introduction, methodology, results, discussion, and conclusion.
- Use headings and subheadings: Organize your content into clear sections with headings and subheadings.
- Use bullet points and numbered lists: Break down complex information into smaller, digestible chunks.

**4. Write Clear and Concise Content:**

- Use simple language: Avoid jargon and technical terms that may confuse your audience.
- Write in active voice: Use active voice to make your writing more engaging.
- Proofread carefully: Check for errors in grammar, spelling, and punctuation.

**5. Use Visual Aids Effectively:**

- Charts and graphs: Use charts and graphs to visualize data and trends.
- Images and diagrams: Use images and diagrams to illustrate complex concepts.
- Tables: Use tables to organize and present data in a clear and concise manner.

**6. Cite Your Sources:**

- Use a consistent citation style: Choose a citation style (e.g., APA, MLA, Chicago) and use it consistently throughout your report.
- Provide accurate citations: Include all necessary information, such as author names, publication dates, and page numbers.

**7. Edit and Proofread:**

- Review your content: Read your report carefully to ensure that it is clear, concise, and well-organized.
- Get feedback: Ask a colleague or friend to review your report and provide feedback.
- Proofread carefully: Check for errors in grammar, spelling, and punctuation.

By following these steps, you can develop high-quality content that is informative, engaging, and easy to understand.

**What to Avoid in Project Report Writing**

While it's important to include essential information in your project report, there are certain elements that should be avoided:

**1. Irrelevant Information:**

- Avoid including excessive details that do not contribute to the main points of the report.
- Stay focused on the core topic and avoid discussing unrelated subjects.

**2. Poor Organization:**

- A disorganized report can be difficult to follow and understand.
- Use consistent formatting throughout the report for headings, font styles, and spacing.

**3. Weak Writing Style:**

- Avoid using overly complex language or jargon that may confuse the reader.
- Use active voice to make your writing more direct and engaging.

- Errors in grammar and punctuation can detract from the credibility of your report.

**4. Lack of Clarity and Conciseness:**

- Use concise language and avoid unnecessary words or phrases.
- Break down complex sentences into simpler ones to improve readability.

**5. Inadequate Visuals:**

- Use high-quality images and graphs that are clear and easy to understand.
- Avoid cluttering your report with too many visuals.

**6. Insufficient Data Analysis:**

- Provide a thorough analysis of the data, including both quantitative and qualitative insights.
- Support your claims with evidence and data.

**7. Weak Conclusion:**

- Avoid simply restating the findings.
- **Lack of Recommendations:** Provide actionable recommendations based on the findings.

These pitfalls, you can create a well-structured, informative, and engaging project report. Remember to proofread carefully and seek feedback from others to ensure the quality of your work.

# TWENTY-ONE
# ACKNOWLEDGEMENT

Acknowledgments are a crucial section of a project report where you express gratitude to individuals, organizations, or institutions that have contributed to the project's success. This can include:

**Mentors and Supervisors**

- **Guidance:** They provide direction, advice, and expertise to help you navigate the project.
- **Support:** They offer emotional encouragement, problem-solving assistance, and feedback.
- **Expertise:** They share their knowledge and experience to help you overcome challenges and make informed decisions.

**Funding Agencies**

- **Financial support:** They provide the necessary funds to carry out the project.
- **Resources:** They may also offer additional resources like equipment, facilities, or connections.
- **Oversight:** They may monitor the project's progress and ensure that funds are used appropriately.

**Collaborators**

- **Teamwork:** They work together with you on the project, sharing their skills and perspectives.

- **Problem-solving**: They contribute to finding solutions to challenges and making progress.
- **Knowledge sharing:** They help to expand your knowledge and understanding of the project's subject matter.

**Technical or Administrative Staff**

- **Support services:** They provide essential services like IT support, administrative assistance, or technical expertise.
- **Efficiency:** They help to streamline processes and ensure that the project runs smoothly.
- **Problem-solving:** They assist with resolving technical or logistical issues.

**Family and Friends**

- **Emotional support:** They offer encouragement, understanding, and a listening ear.
- **Practical assistance:** They may help with tasks like childcare, transportation, or household chores.
- **Motivation:** They provide a positive influence and help you stay motivated throughout the project.

**Guidelines for Writing Acknowledgments**

1. **Identify Key Contributors:**

    - Acknowledge the guidance and support provided by your mentors or supervisors.
    - Recognize the contributions of any team members or collaborators.
    - Thank any organizations or individuals who have provided financial support.
    - Acknowledge the resources and facilities provided by your institution.

2. **Be Specific and Sincere:**

    - Highlight specific contributions: Mention the ways in which individuals have helped your project.

   - Express genuine gratitude: Convey your appreciation for the support you have received.

3. **Maintain a Professional Tone:**

   - Avoid overly personal language: Keep your acknowledgment formal and professional.
   - Proofread carefully: Ensure that there are no errors in grammar or spelling.

4. **Consider Cultural Norms:**

Be mindful of cultural differences: If you are working with individuals from different cultures, be aware of their customs and expectations regarding acknowledgments.

**Example Acknowledgment**

"I would like to express my sincere gratitude to my supervisor, Dr. [Supervisor's Name], for his invaluable guidance and support throughout this project. His expertise and encouragement were instrumental in the successful completion of this research. I would also like to thank my colleagues, [Collaborator's Names], for their valuable contributions and collaborative spirit. Additionally, I am grateful to the [Funding Agency] for their financial support, which made this research possible."

**The Role of Acknowledgements in a Project Report**

An acknowledgement section in a project report is a crucial part where you express gratitude to individuals and organizations who contributed to the completion of your project. It's a gesture of professional courtesy and recognition.

**Key Roles of Acknowledgements:**

1. **Expressing Gratitude:**

   - Personal Thanks: Acknowledge the support and guidance of mentors, advisors, and colleagues.
   - Institutional Thanks: Thank organizations, institutions, or funding agencies that provided resources or facilities.

- Family and Friends: Express appreciation for their emotional support and encouragement.

2. **Recognizing Contributions:**

   - Specific Contributions: Highlight the specific contributions of individuals, such as data collection, analysis, or technical assistance.
   - Collective Efforts: Acknowledge the collaborative efforts of a team or group.

3. **Maintaining Professional Relationships:**

   - Building Goodwill: Show appreciation for the support received and strengthen professional relationships.
   - Ethical Considerations: Acknowledge any ethical guidelines or regulations followed during the project.

4. **Academic Integrity:**

   - Attribution: Give credit to the original sources of information and ideas.
   - Avoiding Plagiarism: Demonstrate your commitment to academic honesty and integrity.

**BENEFITS OF ACKNOWLEDGEMENTS IN PROJECT REPORT WRITING**

Acknowledgements in a project report serve several important purposes:

1. **Professional Courtesy:**

   - Shows Gratitude: Expressing gratitude to those who contributed to the project fosters positive relationships.
   - Recognizes Contributions: Acknowledging specific contributions highlights the value of individual efforts.

2. **Ethical Responsibility:**

- Gives Credit: Assigning credit to those who deserve it upholds academic integrity.
- Avoiding Plagiarism: Explicitly acknowledging sources prevents plagiarism and intellectual dishonesty.

3. **Building Professional Networks:**

    - Strengthening Relationships: Acknowledging others can lead to future collaborations and opportunities.
    - Expanding Professional Circles: Connecting with new individuals and institutions can broaden your network.

4. **Enhancing Project Credibility:**

    - Transparency: Demonstrating transparency and honesty in recognizing contributions.
    - Building Trust: Fostering trust with readers by acknowledging the support received.

5. **Personal Satisfaction:**

    - Sense of Fulfillment: Expressing gratitude can bring a sense of satisfaction and closure.
    - Motivation: Recognizing the support of others can motivate future endeavors.

By including a thoughtful acknowledgement section in your project report, you can enhance its overall impact and demonstrate your professionalism and integrity.

# TWENTY-TWO
# FUNDING DETAILS

Funding details are essential for transparency and accountability in a project report. They provide information about the financial resources that supported the project and how those funds were used.

**Here are some key elements to include in your funding details section:**

**Key Information to Include**

**1.Funding Sources:**

Clearly identify all sources of funding. This could include:

- Government grants
- Private donations
- Corporate sponsorships
- In-kind contributions
- Internal funding (e.g., from an organization's own resources)

Specify the amount contributed by each source.

**2. Funding Amounts:**

- Provide the total funding amount allocated to the project.
- Break down the amounts by funding source, if applicable.
- Indicate any changes in funding amounts during the project's lifetime (e.g., additional funding or budget cuts).

**3. Funding Disbursement:**

- Describe how the funds were disbursed (e.g., in installments, lump sums).
- Explain any specific conditions or requirements attached to the funding.

**4. Financial Management:**

- Outline the financial management procedures used to track and control project expenditures.
- Mention any financial oversight bodies or committees involved.
- Discuss any auditing or financial reviews conducted.

**5. Budget vs. Actual Expenditures:**

- Present a comparison of the project's original budget with the actual expenditures.
- Highlight any significant variances and provide explanations for them.

**6. Financial Reporting:**

- Describe the frequency and format of financial reports submitted to funding agencies or internal stakeholders.
- Specify who is responsible for preparing and reviewing these reports.

**Example Funding Details Section**
**Funding Sources:**

- Government Grant from the Ministry of Science and Technology: INR 2,500,000
- Corporate Sponsorship from XYZ Corporation: INR 1,000,000

**Funding Disbursement:**

- The government grant was disbursed in two installments: 50% upfront and 50% upon completion of the first phase.
- The corporate sponsorship was provided as a lump sum at the project's commencement.

**Financial Management:**

- A dedicated project accountant is responsible for tracking and managing project finances.

- Monthly financial reports are submitted to the funding agencies and the project steering committee.

**Budget vs. Actual Expenditures:**

- The project has remained within budget, with a slight underspending of INR 50,000 due to cost-saving measures.

By providing detailed information about funding sources, amounts, disbursement, and management, you enhance the credibility and transparency of your project report.

**2. Funding Details in Project Report and types of Funding Details.**

**Introduction**

When it comes to crafting a project report, one of the most crucial sections is undoubtedly the funding details. It holds the smart glue that connects your project's vision with the monetary support it requires to take flight. So, let's dive into what makes funding details significant and how to present them clearly and effectively.

**Why Funding Details Matter**

**The Backbone of Your Project**

Funding details are not just a list of expenses; they encapsulate the financial plan that supports your entire project. Think of it as your project's backbone— without a solid support system, things can quickly go awry.

**Building Trust with Stakeholders**

When potential investors or stakeholders read your report, they want clarity and transparency. Providing well-structured funding details builds trust. It shows them that you understand the financial aspects of your project and assures them that their investment will be managed wisely.

**Types of Funding Sources**

**Government Grants**

Government grants can be a golden ticket for many projects, especially non-profits. In my experience applying for a local community project, the grant application process was lengthy, but well worth the effort.

- **Pros:** No repayment required, and it often comes with additional resources or training.
- **Cons:** Strict eligibility criteria and extensive reporting requirements can be daunting.

**Private Investors**

Private investors can bring not just funds but also expertise and networking opportunities. I once collaborated with a startup that secured a private angel investor; their insights propelled us forward in ways we hadn't imagined!

- **Pros:** Flexible funding arrangements and quick access to capital.
- **Cons:** You may have to give up a portion of ownership or profits.

**Crowdfunding**

Crowdfunding has become increasingly popular thanks to platforms like Kickstarter and GoFundMe. It's not just about fundraising; it's about community building!

- **Pros:** Engages your audience and raises awareness for your project.
- **Cons:** Success is not guaranteed; campaigns require significant marketing effort.

**Loans**

For many ambitious entrepreneurs, loans can be a viable option. I remember the mixed emotions when I took out a small business loan—excitement for the potential and a knot in my stomach for the obligations.

- **Pros:** Retain full control over your project.
- **Cons:** Repayment can be a stress factor, particularly if revenues don't flow as expected.

**Presenting the Funding Details**

**Breakdown of Project Costs**

When outlining funding details, it's vital to provide a clear itemization of all costs. This should ideally cover:

- **Personnel Costs:** Salaries, benefits, and any consultants or freelancers you might employ.
- **Material Costs:** What resources will you need, and how much will they cost.

- **Operational Costs:** Rent, utilities, and other ongoing expenses that keep your project running.

This past summer, I worked on a small event project where we meticulously broke down every little cost, from refreshments to venue fees, and it really helped us stay on track financially.

**Timeline for Funding**

Providing a timeline showing when funds will be required and how they will be deployed throughout the project's lifecycle can be immensely helpful. It gives stakeholders a sense of control and assurance.

**Funding Goals**

Clearly stating your funding goals and what milestones trigger additional funding needs can be a game changer. It helps in aligning expectations; for example, "By month six, we should have raised 70% of our total budget to proceed to phase two."

**Conclusion**

Taking the time to prepare thorough and transparent funding details in your project report can open doors, foster trust, and lay the groundwork for successful financial management. Whether you're a seasoned project manager or stepping into this world for the first time, understanding funding details sets a strong foundation for your aspirations. Don't forget to keep refining and adjusting your funding details as your project evolves. Every detail counts, and you never know who might be reading your report.

# TWENTY-THREE
# ABSTRACT

An abstract is a concise summary of your project report, typically around 150-250 words. It should provide a clear overview of the entire project, including:

Background/Introduction: Briefly introduce the topic and its significance.

Problem/Objective: Clearly state the problem or research question your project addresses.

Methodology/Approach: Describe the methods or techniques used to conduct the research.

Findings/Results: Summarize the key findings or outcomes of your project.

Conclusion: Present the main conclusions drawn from the results.

**Key Points to Remember:**

Conciseness: Keep it brief and to the point.

Clarity: Use clear and concise language.

Completeness: Cover all essential aspects of the project.

Self-contained: It should be understandable without reading the full report.

Keywords: Include relevant keywords to aid in indexing and searching.

Structure:

While the structure can vary slightly depending on the field, a common approach is to follow the IMRaD format:

Introduction: Briefly introduce the topic and research question.

Methods: Summarize the research methodology and data collection techniques.

Results: Highlight the key findings and results.

Discussion/Conclusion: Interpret the results and draw conclusions.

Placement:

The abstract is usually placed at the beginning of the report, after the title page and before the table of contents.

# TWENTY-FOUR
# INTRODUCTION

The introduction is the first section of your project report and sets the stage for the rest of your work. It should be engaging, informative, and well-structured.

Key Components of an Introduction:

Background:

Context: Provide a brief overview of the broader context of your project.

Problem Statement: Clearly articulate the specific problem or issue your project aims to address.

Research Gap: Highlight the gap in existing knowledge or understanding that your project seeks to fill.

Objective:

Research Question(s): State the specific questions your research will answer.

Research Aim: Outline the overall goal of your research.

Scope:

Boundaries: Define the limits and parameters of your research.

Focus Areas: Specify the specific areas your research will cover.

Methodology:

Research Approach: Briefly describe the overall approach (e.g., qualitative, quantitative, mixed-methods).

Data Collection Methods: Outline the techniques used to gather data (e.g., surveys, interviews, experiments).

Data Analysis Techniques: Explain the methods used to analyze the data (e.g., statistical analysis, thematic analysis).

Report Organization:

Structure: Provide a brief overview of the structure of the report, indicating the main sections and their purpose.

Example Introduction Draft 1:

The rapid advancement of technology has revolutionized various aspects of human life, including education. However, the integration of technology in traditional classrooms has not been without challenges. This project aims to investigate the impact of technology-enhanced learning on student engagement and academic performance in high school mathematics. Specifically, the study will explore the effectiveness of using interactive online platforms and virtual reality simulations in enhancing student learning experiences. By examining these factors, this research seeks to provide valuable insights for educators and policymakers to optimize the use of technology in education.

Example Introduction Draft 2:

Climate change poses a significant threat to global sustainability. Rising sea levels, extreme weather events, and biodiversity loss are just a few of the consequences of unchecked carbon emissions. This project focuses on analyzing the impact of climate change on coastal ecosystems, particularly in [specific region]. By examining historical data, conducting field surveys, and utilizing climate modeling techniques, this study aims to assess the vulnerability of coastal ecosystems to climate change and identify potential adaptation strategies. The findings of this research will contribute to informed decision-making and sustainable coastal management practices.

# TWENTY-FIVE
# AIM OF THE STUDY

The primary aim of this study is to [clearly state the overall goal of the research]. Specifically, this research aims to:

- Objective 1: [Specific objective related to the main goal]
- Objective 2: [Specific objective related to the main goal]
- Objective 3: [Specific objective related to the main goal]

By achieving these objectives, we hope to [describe the potential impact of the research, such as advancing knowledge, improving practices, or informing policy].

**For example:**

If your research is about the impact of climate change on coastal ecosystems:

The aim of this study is to assess the impact of climate change on coastal ecosystems. Specifically, this research aims to:

- Objective 1: Quantify the rate of coastal erosion due to sea-level rise.
- Objective 2: Evaluate the impact of climate change on biodiversity in coastal ecosystems.
- Objective 3: Develop adaptation strategies to mitigate the effects of climate change on coastal communities.

By achieving these objectives, we hope to provide valuable insights to policymakers and coastal communities to develop effective adaptation and mitigation strategies.

# TWENTY-SIX

# BACKGROUND

Provide a brief overview of the current state of knowledge or the problem you are addressing. Briefly describe the existing research gap or the need for your proposed research. Highlight the significance of the research problem and why it is worth investigating.

**Example:**

[If your research is about climate change and its impact on agriculture]

Climate change poses a significant threat to global food security. Rising temperatures, altered precipitation patterns, and increased frequency of extreme weather events are disrupting agricultural production worldwide. Despite these challenges, there is a lack of comprehensive research on the specific impacts of climate change on [specific crop or region].

The background section of a project report provides essential context for understanding the project's purpose, significance, and the rationale behind its undertaking. It sets the stage for the rest of the report and helps readers grasp the broader context in which the project operates.

**KEY ELEMENTS TYPICALLY INCLUDED IN THE BACKGROUND SECTION:**

Problem Statement: Clearly articulates the issue or challenge that the project aims to address.

Project Objectives: Outlines the specific goals and outcomes the project intends to achieve.

Significance and Impact: Explains why the project is important and how it will contribute to a particular field, industry, or community.

Existing Knowledge or Research: Summarizes the current state of knowledge or research related to the project topic.

Gaps in Existing Knowledge: Identifies the areas where the project will fill gaps or contribute new insights.

Project Scope: Defines the boundaries and limitations of the project, including what it will and will not cover.

Theoretical Framework: If applicable, explains the theoretical underpinnings or models that guide the project.

**PURPOSE OF THE BACKGROUND SECTION:**

Contextualization: Provides a broader understanding of the project's relevance and significance.

Justification: Explains why the project is necessary and valuable.

Orientation: Guides readers toward the specific focus and objectives of the project.

Foundation: Establishes a solid foundation for the subsequent sections of the report.

**TIPS FOR WRITING A STRONG BACKGROUND SECTION:**

Avoid unnecessary jargon or technical terms that may confuse readers.

Support your claims with relevant data, statistics, or expert opinions.

Demonstrate how the background information relates to the project's goals and objectives.

Stay on topic and avoid tangents that are not directly relevant to the project.

Ensure that the background section is free of errors and inconsistencies.

By providing a well-written and informative background section, you can effectively engage your readers and set the stage for a successful project report.

# TWENTY-SEVEN

# WRITING THE RESEARCH QUESTION

A well-framed research question is the cornerstone of any successful research project. It provides direction, focus, and clarity to your research.

**Key Characteristics of a Good Research Question:**

- It should be easy to understand and free from ambiguity.
- It should be focused on a particular aspect of the research topic.
- It should be achievable within the constraints of your resources and time.
- It should address a significant research gap or problem.
- It should be possible to collect data and analyze it to answer the question.

**Steps to Develop a Strong Research Question:**

**1. Identify Your Research Topic:**

- Choose a topic that genuinely interests you to maintain motivation.
- Select a topic that is relevant to current issues or has practical applications.
- Consider the resources, time, and expertise required to conduct the research.

**2. Brainstorm Ideas:**

- Write down any ideas that come to mind, without judgment.
- Visually map out concepts and ideas.

- Explore existing research to identify gaps and opportunities.

**3. Refine Your Question:**

- Narrow down your topic to a specific aspect.
- Use simple, direct language to avoid ambiguity.
- Ensure that your question can be answered with available resources and methods.
- Consider any ethical implications of your research question.

**4. Consult with Experts:**

- Get input from professors, mentors, or other researchers.
- Anticipate potential obstacles and develop strategies to overcome them.
- Incorporate feedback to strengthen your research question.

**5. Test Your Question:**

- **Ask the 5 Ws:** Who, What, When, Where, Why?
- Why is your research question important?
- How will your research contribute to the field or society?

**Example:**
**Broad Topic:** Climate Change
**Brainstormed Ideas:**

- Impact of climate change on agriculture
- Climate change and sea-level rise
- Renewable energy solutions
- Climate change policies and regulations

**Refined Research Question:**

- How does climate change affect agricultural productivity in [specific region]?

Example:
Topic: The impact of climate change on coastal ecosystems

Broad Research Question: How does climate change affect coastal ecosystems?

Refined Research Question: What is the impact of sea-level rise on coastal erosion rates in [specific region]?

By refining your research question, you can ensure that your research is focused and that your findings are meaningful.

**To write a compelling research question for your project report, consider the following steps:**

1. Define your research topic: Clearly identify the subject matter you want to investigate.
2. Identify the problem or gap in knowledge: Determine what is missing or unclear about your topic.
3. Ask a specific and focused question: Frame your question in a way that seeks a clear answer.
4. Make it researchable: Ensure your question can be answered through empirical investigation.
5. Consider the scope: Define the boundaries of your research to make it manageable.
6. Use clear and concise language: Avoid jargon or overly complex phrasing.
7. Align with your research objectives: Make sure your question contributes to achieving your overall goals.

**Tips to develop Research questions**

- Avoid asking yes/no questions.
- Be specific about the variables you want to investigate.
- Consider the potential implications of your research.
- Seek feedback from others to refine your question.

# TWENTY-EIGHT

# NEED OF THE STUDY/ PROJECT SIGNIFICANCE

The "need of the study" or "project significance" section of a research proposal or report is crucial. It outlines why your research is important, relevant, and worth pursuing. It answers the question: "Why is this research necessary?"

**Key Components to Address:**

1. **Identifying the Problem or Gap:**
    - Clearly articulate the problem or research question: What specific issue or knowledge gap does your research aim to address?
    - Highlight the significance of the problem: Explain why this problem is important and how it affects individuals, society, or a specific field.
2. **Explaining the Significance:**
    - Theoretical Significance: How will your research contribute to existing theories or knowledge in your field? Will it challenge existing paradigms or propose new ones?
    - Practical Significance: How will your research be applied in real-world settings? Can it lead to the development of new technologies, policies, or practices?

- Social Impact: How will your research benefit society? Will it improve people's lives, address social issues, or inform public policy?

3. **Justifying the Research:**

   - Novelty: Explain how your research is original and adds to the existing body of knowledge.
   - Feasibility: Demonstrate that your research is achievable within the given resources and timeframe.
   - Ethical Considerations: Address any ethical implications of your research and how you will mitigate them.

**Example:**
**Research Topic: The Impact of Climate Change on Coastal Ecosystems**
Need of the Study:

Climate change poses a significant threat to coastal ecosystems worldwide. Rising sea levels, increased storm intensity, and ocean acidification are causing severe damage to coastal habitats and biodiversity. This study aims to assess the vulnerability of coastal ecosystems to climate change and develop strategies for their conservation and restoration.

By addressing this research gap, we will:

- Improve our understanding of the complex interactions between climate change and coastal ecosystems.
- Provide valuable information to policymakers and coastal managers for developing effective adaptation and mitigation strategies.
- Contribute to the development of sustainable coastal management practices.

**Significant**

- The significance of your research will vary depending on your specific topic and research questions.
- Support your claims with relevant data, statistics, and expert opinions.
- Avoid jargon and technical terms that may confuse your audience.
- Explain how your research can make a difference in the real world.

Effectively communicating the need and significance of your research, you can increase the likelihood of securing funding and support for your project.

# TWENTY-NINE
# RELEVANCE

The relevance of a research project is crucial. It determines its impact, its potential to contribute to existing knowledge, and its practical applications. A relevant research project should:

**Address a Significant Problem or Question**

- Clearly articulate the gap in existing knowledge or the problem that needs to be addressed.
- Explain why this problem is important and how it affects individuals, society, or a specific field.

**Contribute to the Field of Study**

- Expand the existing body of knowledge by providing new insights or theories.
- Question conventional wisdom and offer alternative perspectives.
- Provide evidence-based recommendations to inform policy decisions or improve practices.

**Have Practical Applications**

- Demonstrate how the research findings can be applied to solve real-world problems.
- Highlight the potential social, economic, or environmental benefits of the research.

**Consider Ethical Implications**

- Ensure that the research is conducted ethically and responsibly.
- Protect the rights and well-being of research participants.

# THIRTY

# DETERMINING THE FEASIBILITY

Feasibility refers to the practicality of conducting a research project. It involves assessing whether the project can be completed within the given constraints, such as time, budget, and resources.

**Key Factors to Consider:**

1. **Time Constraints:**

    - Project Timeline: Develop a realistic timeline for each stage of the research process, from literature review to data analysis and report writing.
    - Time Commitment: Assess the time required for data collection, analysis, and interpretation.
    - Deadlines: Consider any external deadlines or milestones that may impact the project timeline.

2. **Resource Constraints:**

    - Financial Resources: Determine the budget required for the project, including equipment, software, supplies, and personnel costs.
    - Human Resources: Assess the availability of skilled researchers, technicians, or other personnel.
    - Infrastructure: Consider the availability of necessary infrastructure, such as laboratories, libraries, or computing facilities.

3. **Data Accessibility:**

   - Data Sources: Identify reliable and accessible data sources.
   - Data Quality: Evaluate the quality and relevance of the available data.
   - Data Collection Methods: Determine the feasibility of data collection methods, such as surveys, interviews, or experiments.

4. **Ethical Considerations:**

   - Ethical Approval: Ensure that the research complies with ethical guidelines and regulations.
   - Participant Consent: Obtain informed consent from participants, if applicable.
   - Data Privacy: Protect the privacy and confidentiality of participants.

5. **Technical Feasibility:**

   - Methodology: Choose appropriate research methodologies and techniques.
   - Statistical Analysis: Ensure that the necessary statistical tools and software are available.
   - Data Analysis Skills: Assess the researcher's skills and expertise in data analysis.

**Example:**
**Research Topic: The Impact of Climate Change on Coastal Ecosystems**
Feasibility Considerations:

- Time Constraints: The project may require long-term monitoring and data collection, which could impact the timeline.
- Resource Constraints: Access to coastal field sites, specialized equipment, and expert personnel may be limited.
- Data Accessibility: Historical climate data and ecological data may be difficult to obtain and analyze.
- Ethical Considerations: Obtaining permits for fieldwork and ensuring the ethical treatment of ecosystems and organisms.
- Technical Feasibility: The use of remote sensing techniques and geographic information systems (GIS) may require specialized training

and software.

By carefully considering these factors, researchers can assess the feasibility of their project and make informed decisions about its scope and timeline.

# THIRTY-ONE

# THEORETICAL FRAMEWORK

A theoretical framework provides a structured approach to understanding a research problem. It outlines the theories, concepts, and models that will guide your research. By developing a strong theoretical framework, you can ensure that your research is grounded in existing knowledge and provides a clear rationale for your research questions and hypotheses.

**Key Components of a Theoretical Framework:**

1. **Core Concepts:**
   - Identify the key concepts that are central to your research.
   - Define these concepts clearly and concisely.
   - Explain how these concepts relate to your research problem.

2. **Theoretical Foundations:**
   - Review relevant theories and models from your field of study.
   - Select the most appropriate theories to guide your research.
   - Explain how these theories will help you understand your research problem.

3. **Conceptual Framework:**
   - Develop a conceptual framework that visually represents the relationships between the key variables in your study.

- Use diagrams or models to illustrate the theoretical underpinnings of your research.

4. **Research Questions and Hypotheses:**

   - Formulate clear and specific research questions based on your theoretical framework.
   - Develop testable hypotheses that can be empirically verified.

**Example:**

**Research Topic: The Impact of Social Media on Adolescent Mental Health**

**Theoretical Framework:**

- Social Cognitive Theory: This theory explains how people learn through observation and imitation. In the context of social media, adolescents may learn negative behaviors or attitudes from their peers.
- Self-Determination Theory: This theory emphasizes the importance of autonomy, competence, and relatedness for psychological well-being. Social media can impact these needs, leading to positive or negative outcomes.
- Stress and Coping Theory: This theory explains how individuals cope with stress and adversity. Social media can be a source of stress, but it can also be used as a coping mechanism.

**Conceptual Framework:**

conceptual framework showing the relationships between social media use, psychological wellbeing, and the mediating role of social cognitive theory, self determination theory, and stress and coping theory

**Research Questions:**

1. How does social media use impact adolescent self-esteem and body image?
2. What are the relationships between social media use, sleep quality, and academic performance among adolescents?
3. How do adolescents use social media to cope with stress and anxiety?

A strong theoretical framework, you can ensure that your research is grounded in theory, methodologically sound, and contributes to the existing body of knowledge.

**Advantages of a Strong Theoretical Framework**

**A well-developed theoretical framework offers several advantages:**

- It provides a clear focus for your research, guiding your research questions and hypotheses.
- It helps you understand the underlying mechanisms and processes that influence your research topic.
- It ensures that your research methods are appropriate and rigorous.
- It enhances the credibility and rigor of your research by grounding it in established theories.
- It allows you to contribute to the existing body of knowledge by building on existing theories or developing new ones.
- It can inform policy decisions and practical applications by providing evidence-based insights.

**Disadvantages of a Weak Theoretical Framework**

A weak or poorly developed theoretical framework can lead to several disadvantages:

- Without a clear theoretical foundation, your research may lack direction and focus.
- A weak theoretical framework can lead to methodological weaknesses, such as inappropriate research designs or data analysis techniques.
- A weak theoretical framework may limit your ability to interpret your findings and draw meaningful conclusions.
- A poorly developed theoretical framework can undermine the credibility of your research.
- A weak theoretical framework may limit the impact of your research by failing to address significant research questions or provide practical insights.

**To avoid these pitfalls, it is essential to:**

- Thoroughly review the existing literature to identify relevant theories and concepts.

- Choose theories that are relevant to your research question and can provide a strong foundation for your study.
- Clearly Define Concepts: Clearly define the key concepts and variables in your study.
- Develop a Logical Framework: Create a logical and coherent framework that links your theoretical concepts to your research questions and hypotheses.
- Test Your Framework: Ensure that your framework is testable and can be empirically verified.

# THIRTY-TWO
# LITERATURE REVIEW

A literature review is a critical evaluation of existing research on a specific topic. It establishes a framework for understanding the current state of knowledge and identifies gaps for future research. This presentation explores the methodology and framework necessary for effective project reporting. A literature review is a critical assessment of the body of existing research relevant to a specific topic or field of study.

It involves summarizing, analyzing, and synthesizing the findings of various sources such as books, articles, and papers, in order to identify gaps, inconsistencies, or trends in the research. The primary goal is to provide a comprehensive overview of what is already known about a topic, and how that knowledge has evolved over time.

**IMPORTANCE OF A LITERATURE REVIEW**

1. **Establishes Context:** It helps place your own research within the larger body of work in the field, providing a clear context for why your research is necessary or relevant.
2. **Identifies Gaps:** A good literature review highlights what is still unknown or under-researched, enabling you to identify opportunities for further study or to address specific gaps in the literature.
3. **Avoids Duplication:** By reviewing existing research, you ensure that your study does not replicate work that has already been done, unless replication is a part of your methodology.
4. **Supports Methodology:** It can inform your choice of research methods by demonstrating which techniques have been effective or problematic in previous studies.

5. **Enhances Credibility:** Demonstrating a thorough understanding of the literature establishes your credibility and expertise on the subject.
6. **Guides Future Research:** A well-conducted literature review can act as a roadmap for future researchers, pointing out promising areas for new investigations.

## PURPOSE OF LITERATURE REVIEW

The main **purpose** of a literature review is to summarize and synthesize existing research. It helps to contextualize the study within the broader academic dialogue. A well-structured review informs **project reporting** by providing a solid foundation for the research objectives and methodology.

The **purpose of a literature survey** (also called a literature review) is multifaceted. It serves as a foundational component of a research project, helping to position your work within the broader academic context and ensuring that your study is well-informed by existing knowledge.

### 1. Understanding the Research Landscape

- It helps in identifying what has already been studied, the theories or models used, and the methods that have been applied.

### 2. Identifying Gaps in the Literature

- One of the primary goals of the literature review is to uncover gaps, inconsistencies, or limitations in the current research. These gaps might be theoretical, methodological, or empirical.

### 3. Avoiding Duplication

- If someone has already addressed your research problem comprehensively, repeating the same study without adding new value would be redundant.

## METHODOLOGY:

The **methodology** of a literature review involves systematic searching, data extraction, and critical appraisal of selected studies. Utilizing a structured approach ensures that the review is **objective** and replicable, enhancing the credibility of the project report and its findings

## APPROACHES TO THE STRUCTURING OF LITERATURE REVIEW

**Thematic:** In a thematic outline, you will organize your information around a single therne

Chronological: This method allows you to demonstrate the evolution of your topic across time

Methodological: In this style, you will examine the various research methodologies employed by your sources

Theoretical: A theoretical framework allows you to concentrate on explaining the various models, ideas, and essential concepts

**Benefits of a Literature Review**

A literature review is a crucial step in the research process. It helps you gain a comprehensive understanding of the existing knowledge on your research topic. Here are some key benefits of conducting a thorough literature review:

- Knowledge Base
- Research Question Development
- Methodology Development
- Ethical Considerations
- Enhancing the Quality of Your Research

By conducting a thorough literature review, you can lay a strong foundation for your research, improve the quality of your work, and contribute to the advancement of knowledge in your field.

# THIRTY-THREE
# RESEARCH DESIGN

A research design is a comprehensive framework that outlines the methodology and procedures for collecting, analyzing, and interpreting data in a research study. It serves as the blueprint for conducting research, ensuring that the research question is addressed effectively and efficiently. Research design plays a critical role in the validity, reliability, and overall success of the research project.

**Elements of Research Design**

**1. Research Problem or Question:** The research design is built around the central research question or hypothesis that the study seeks to answer or test.

**2. Purpose of the Study:** Determines whether the research is exploratory, descriptive, explanatory, or evaluative in nature.

**3. Variables and Hypotheses:** Identifies the independent and dependent variables, as well as any control variables. Hypotheses, if applicable, guide the study in terms of what relationships or effects are being examined.

**4. Sampling Strategy:** Defines how participants or subjects will be selected, including sample size, sampling method (random, stratified, etc.), and the target population.

**5. Data Collection Methods:** Describes the techniques for gathering data, such as surveys, interviews, experiments, or observations.

**6. Data Analysis Techniques:** Outlines the methods for analyzing the data, such as statistical tests, content analysis, or thematic analysis. It also includes the software or tools that will be used in the analysis.

**7. Time Frame:** Describes whether the study will be cross-sectional (data collected at one point in time) or longitudinal (data collected over an extended period).

**8. Ethical Considerations:** Ensures that the research design accounts for ethical concerns, such as informed consent, confidentiality, and the protection of participants from harm.

**9. Validity and Reliability:** Focuses on ensuring that the research results are credible (valid) and consistent (reliable).

**Types of Research Design**

**Exploratory Research Design:**

Used when little is known about the topic, and the researcher seeks to explore new insights or generate hypotheses. Methods like interviews or focus groups are common.

**Descriptive Research Design:**

Aims to describe characteristics of a population or phenomenon. It answers the "what" question but not the "why" or "how." Surveys and observational studies are typical methods.

**Explanatory Research Design:**

Focuses on identifying cause-and-effect relationships. Experimental research, including randomized controlled trials (RCTs), is an example.

**4. Experimental Research Design:**

Involves manipulating one variable to determine its effect on another variable. This design includes both true experiments (with random assignment) and quasi-experiments (without random assignment).

**5. Correlational Research Design:**

Examines relationships between variables without manipulating them. It identifies associations but does not establish causality.

**6. Case Study Research Design:**

Involves an in-depth analysis of a single case or a small number of cases, often used in qualitative research to explore complex issues.

**Steps in Research Design for a Project Report**

A well-structured research design is crucial for conducting a successful research project. Here are the key steps involved in research design:

**1. Define the Research Problem:**

- Clearly articulate the specific question or problem that your research aims to address.
- Break down the research question into smaller, specific objectives.

**2. Review the Literature:**

- Examine existing research to identify gaps in knowledge.
- Select relevant theories to underpin your research.
- Construct a conceptual framework that guides your research.

**3. Formulate Research Hypotheses or Research Questions:**

- Create specific, measurable, and testable hypotheses.
- If a hypothesis-testing approach is not suitable, formulate clear and focused research questions.

**4. Choose a Research Design:**

- Choose a research design that best fits your research question and objectives.
- **Consider the Following Designs:**
    - Manipulating variables to observe their effects.
    - Similar to experimental design but lacks random assignment.
    - Collecting data through questionnaires or interviews.
    - In-depth analysis of a specific case or phenomenon.
    - Examining relationships between variables.

**5. Develop the Research Instrument:**

- Develop instruments like questionnaires, interview guides, or observation checklists.
- Validate the instruments to ensure they measure what they intend to measure.

**6. Determine the Sample Size and Sampling Technique:**

- Determine the appropriate sample size based on the research design and statistical power analysis.
- Choose a suitable sampling technique (e.g., random sampling, stratified sampling, purposive sampling).

**7. Data Collection Procedures:**

- Outline the steps involved in data collection, including timelines and procedures.
- Train data collectors to ensure consistency and accuracy.
- Ensure that data collection adheres to ethical guidelines.

**8. Data Analysis Plan:**

- Choose appropriate statistical or qualitative analysis techniques.
- Outline the steps involved in data cleaning, coding, and analysis.

Following these steps, researchers can ensure that their research is well-designed, rigorous, and capable of generating valid and reliable findings.

**Research Design Examples**

- Experimental Design
- Observational Design
- Survey Design
- Case Study Design
- Action Research
- Content Analysis
- Historical Research
- Longitudinal Study
- Cross-Sectional Survey
- Mixed-Methods Research
- Grounded Theory
- Simulation and Modeling

**Importance of Research Design**

1. **Guides the Research Process:**

It provides a clear plan, ensuring that the research stays focused and structured.

**2. Enhances Validity and Reliability:**

A well-thought-out design ensures that the results of the study are credible and can be replicated.

**3. Helps in Resource Management:**

It assists in organizing resources like time, budget, and manpower efficiently.

**4. Ensures Ethical Research:**

The design accounts for potential ethical issues, ensuring participants' rights and safety are protected.

# THIRTY-FOUR
# METHODS OF DATA COLLECTION

Data collection is a crucial component of research methodology and can be conducted using various methods tailored to the study's objectives. Qualitative methods include interviews, which allow for in-depth, one-on-one conversations to gather detailed insights, and focus groups, where guided discussions among participants can reveal diverse perspectives and group dynamics.

Observations provide a means to systematically note behaviors or events in their natural context, capturing real-world interactions. Content analysis involves examining text or media to identify patterns and themes, offering insights into existing materials. Mixed methods combine both qualitative and quantitative approaches, enriching the research by providing a comprehensive perspective and allowing for triangulation of data. When planning data collection, researchers must consider sampling methods, ensuring ethical standards such as informed consent and confidentiality, and selecting appropriate tools for data collection, like survey platforms or recording devices.

Ultimately, choosing the right methods is essential for obtaining reliable and valid results that can effectively address the research questions.

**METHODS**

1. **Surveys and Questionnaires Description:**

A structured method where participants are asked to respond to a series of questions, usually in written form. These questions can be closed-ended (e.g., multiple choice) or open-ended.

**Advantages:**

- Can reach a large population quickly.
- Easy to administer online, by mail, or in person. Standardized questions provide consistency in responses.

**Disadvantages:**

- Limited depth of responses.
- Response bias (participants may not answer truthfully).

**Example:** Customer satisfaction surveys after a purchase.

**2. Interviews Description:**

A method of collecting data through direct, face-to-face interaction, telephone, or video calls. Interviews can be structured (predefined set of questions), semi-structured (flexible questions), or unstructured (conversational).

**Advantages:**

- Allows for in-depth responses and clarifications.
- Useful for exploring complex issues.

**Disadvantages:**

- Time-consuming and labor-intensive.
- Potential interviewer bias.

**Example:**

Interviews with experts in a field to gain deeper insights into their experiences or opinions.

**3. Observations Description:**

Involves watching participants or phenomena in a natural or controlled environment and recording relevant data. Observations can be direct or indirect

**Advantages:**

- Captures real-time data in natural settings.

- Useful for behavioral studies.

**Disadvantages:**

- Observer bias may affect data accuracy.
- Participants may alter their behavior when they know they are being observed (Hawthorne effect).

**Example:**

Observing children's interactions in a playground to study social behavior.

**4. Experiments Description:**

A method where the researcher manipulates one or more variables (independent variables) and observes the effect on another variable (dependent variable). Experiments can be done in controlled environments (lab) or in the field.

**Advantages:**

- Can establish cause-and-effect relationships.
- High level of control over variables.

**Disadvantages:**

- Results may not always apply to real-world settings.
- Ethical constraints may limit certain types of experimentation.

**Example:**

Testing the effectiveness of a new drug in a clinical trial

**5. Focus Groups Description:**

A qualitative method where a small group of participants discuss a particular topic or issue. A moderator facilitates the discussion, and data is collected from participants' interactions and opinions.

**Advantages:**

- Allows for interaction and discussion among participants.
- Can generate new ideas and insights through group dynamics.

**Disadvantages:**

- Difficult to control the direction of the conversation.
- Dominant participants may influence the group's opinions.

**Example:** Focus groups to evaluate consumer preferences for a new product

**6. Secondary Data Collection Description:**

Involves using data that has already been collected by other researchers or organizations, such as government reports, academic papers, and existing datasets.

**Advantages:**

- Saves time and resources since data is already available.
- Access to large, high-quality datasets.

**Disadvantages:**

- Limited control over the quality and accuracy of the data.
- May not perfectly align with the specific research question

**Example:**

Using census data for demographic analysis.

**7. Case Studies Description:**

A detailed and in-depth examination of a single case or a small number of cases within their real-life context. Data is collected through multiple methods, including interviews, observations, and document analysis.

**Advantages:**

- Provides comprehensive and contextual data.
- Useful for studying complex or rare phenomena.

**Disadvantages:**

- Limited generalizability due to the small number of cases.
- Time-consuming.

**Example:**

Analyzing a company's response to a specific crisis.

**8. Document and Archival Research Description:**

Collecting data from existing documents, records, or archival materials.

This can include official reports, historical records, company documents, or academic literature.

**Advantages:**

- Non-intrusive and low-cost.
- Provides historical or longitudinal data.

**Disadvantages:**

- Data may be outdated or incomplete.
- Bias may exist in the way documents were originally produced.

# THIRTY-FIVE

# TOOLS AND PROCEDURES

Tools and Procedures section, various data collection methods will be employed to ensure a comprehensive understanding of the research topic. The primary tool will be structured surveys, designed to capture quantitative data through a combination of closed and open-ended questions.

These surveys will be administered online using platforms such as Google Forms or SurveyMonkey to facilitate efficient distribution and data collection. In addition, semi-structured interviews will be conducted, allowing for in-depth qualitative insights into participants' perspectives.

- These interviews may be conducted face-to-face or via video conferencing tools like Zoom, ensuring flexibility and accessibility.
- Focus groups will also be utilized to foster discussions among participants, enabling the exploration of diverse viewpoints and group dynamics around the research topic.
- Observational methods will complement these approaches by providing real-time data in natural settings, which can reveal behaviors and contexts not captured through self-reported measures.
- The data collection process will include a rigorous preparation phase, involving the development and pilot testing of instruments to ensure clarity and reliability.

Participants will be recruited using a defined sampling strategy, ensuring that informed consent is obtained to respect their rights and privacy.

Throughout the data collection, ethical considerations will be prioritized, including securing ethical approval and implementing measures to maintain participant confidentiality. Collected data will be systematically stored and anonymized to protect participant identities, thus adhering to ethical research standards. This multifaceted approach to data collection will provide a robust foundation for the subsequent analysis and interpretation of findings. Tools and procedures refer to the instruments and processes used to collect, manage, and analyze data during a research study. These can vary widely depending on the research design and objectives. Below is an overview of common tools and procedures used in data collection, analysis, and overall research management.

**DATA COLLECTION**

**Tools:1. Surveys and Questionnaires**

Tools: Online platforms like Google Forms, SurveyMonkey, Qualtrics. Paper-based questionnaires for face-to-face or mailed surveys.

**Procedures:**

- Design the survey with clear, concise questions.
- Choose a sampling method (random, stratified, etc.).
- Distribute the survey and set a timeline for responses.
- Ensure anonymity or confidentiality if required
- Distribute the survey and set a timeline for responses.
- Ensure anonymity or confidentiality if required

**2. Interviews Tools:**

Recording devices (audio or video), notepads for manual note-taking. Software like Zoom, Skype, or Microsoft Teams for remote interviews.

**Procedures:**

- Develop an interview guide or script with open-ended and probing questions.
- Schedule interviews and obtain informed consent from participants.
- Record responses and take notes during or after the interview.
- Transcribe interviews for further analysis.

**3. Observations Tools:**

Observation checklists, tally sheets, or video recording equipment. Software tools like Noldus Observer for coding and analyzing behavior.

**Procedures:**

- Create an observation protocol to specify what behaviors or events to record.
- Observe the participants in natural or controlled environments.
- Record observations systematically and avoid subjective interpretations.

**4. Experiments Tools:**

Lab equipment, sensors, software for running simulations, or online experiment tools like advanced.

**Procedures:**

- Randomly assign participants to control and experimental groups.
- Manipulate the independent variable(s) while keeping other variables constant. Record data on the dependent variable(s) using measurement tools.
- Follow ethical guidelines, especially if working with human participants.

**5. Focus Groups Tools:**

Audio and video recording devices, transcription software. Platforms like Dovetail or Miro for managing focus group data.

**Procedures:**

- Develop a discussion guide for the group.
- Recruit participants and obtain informed consent.
- Facilitate the group discussion, ensuring all participants contribute.
- Record, transcribe, and analyze the discussion data.

**6. Secondary Data Collection Tools:**

Access to databases like PubMed, JSTOR, or government repositories .Reference management tools like Zotero, Mendeley, or EndNote.

**Procedures:**

- Define search criteria (keywords, date range, etc.).
- Collect relevant secondary data from published sources or datasets.
- Organize and critically assess the data for quality and relevance.

**DATA ANALYSIS TOOLS**

1. **Quantitative Data Analysis Tools:**

Statistical software such as SPSS, R, SAS, Stata, or Excel.

**Procedures:**

i. Input the collected data into the statistical software.
v. Perform descriptive analysis (e.g., mean, median) and inferential analysis (e.g., t-tests, regression).
v. Interpret the results in relation to the research hypothesis or question.

**2. Document and File ManagementTools:**

Cloud storage services like Google Drive, Dropbox, or Microsoft OneDrive.

File naming conventions and version control systems.

**Procedures:**

v. Organize files with descriptive names and maintain a clear folder structure.
v. Set permissions for collaborators and establish version control protocols.

**3. Data Cleaning and Preparation Tools:**

Excel, Open Refine, or Python scripts for cleaning datasets.

**Procedures:**

v. Check for missing, duplicate, or erroneous data entries.
v. Standardize formats, such as dates or categories.

## ETHICAL AND PROCEDURAL CONSIDERATIONS

1. **Informed Consent Tools:**

Consent forms (written or digital), online consent platforms like Qualtrics.

**Procedures:**

- Ensure participants understand the purpose, risks, and benefits of the study.
- Obtain their voluntary consent before data collection.

**2. Confidentiality and Anonymity Tools:**

Data encryption tools, anonymization software, and secure databases.

**Procedures:**

- Remove or encrypt personally identifiable information (PII).
- Ensure only authorized personnel have access to sensitive data.

**3. Data Security Tools:**

Security measures like firewalls, encryption software, and password protection.

**Procedures:**

- Follow best practices for data storage, such as encrypting sensitive data.
- Regularly update security protocols to protect against data breaches.

**REPORTING AND PRESENTATION TOOLS:**

**Visualization ToolsTools:**

Tableau, Power BI, Google Data Studio, or Excel for visualizing data.

**Procedures:**

- Create charts, graphs, and dashboards to summarize findings.
- Use visual aids to present data clearly in reports or presentations.

**Report Writing and Documentation Tools:**

Word processors like Microsoft Word or Google Docs, citation management software.

**Procedures:**

- Structure the report logically (introduction, methodology, results, discussion).
- Cite all sources accurately using the appropriate citation style.

**Presentation Tools:**

PowerPoint, Prezi, or Google Slides for creating presentations.

**Procedures:**

- Summarize key findings visually, using clear, concise slides.

- Practice presenting the data and findings to ensure clarity and professionalism.

# THIRTY-SIX
# DATA ANALYSIS

Data Analysis section, the collected data will be systematically processed and interpreted to uncover meaningful patterns and insights. For quantitative data obtained from surveys, statistical analysis will be conducted using software such as SPSS or Excel. Descriptive statistics, including mean, median, and standard deviation, will be calculated to summarize the data and provide a clear overview of key trends.

Inferential statistical tests, such as t-tests or ANOVA, will be employed to examine relationships between variables and assess the significance of findings. For qualitative data gathered from interviews and focus groups, thematic analysis will be utilized.

- This involves transcribing recorded sessions and coding the data to identify recurring themes and patterns. Thematic analysis will allow for a nuanced understanding of participants' experiences and perspectives, highlighting key insights that emerge from the qualitative data.
- A triangulation approach will be adopted to compare and contrast findings from both quantitative and qualitative analyses, ensuring a comprehensive interpretation of the results.
- Data visualization techniques, such as charts and graphs, will be employed to present key findings clearly and effectively. Throughout the analysis process, attention will be paid to ensuring the reliability and validity of the results , including cross-checking findings and incorporating peer debriefing when applicable.

**TYPES OF DATA ANALYSIS:**

**1. Descriptive Analysis:** Summarizes and describes the data.

- Measures of central tendency: Mean, median, mode
- Measures of dispersion: Range, variance, standard deviation

**2. Frequency distributions:** Histograms, bar charts, pie charts

- Inferential Analysis: Makes inferences about a population based on a sample.
- Hypothesis testing: Tests hypotheses about population parameters

**3. Correlation analysis:** Measures the strength and direction of relationships between variables

- Regression analysis: Predicts the value of one variable based on the values of other variables
- Content Analysis: Analyzes qualitative data (e.g., text, images, videos).

**DATA ANALYSIS TOOLS**

- Statistical Software: SPSS, R, SAS, Stata
- Spreadsheets: Excel, Google Sheets
- Data Visualization Tools: Tableau, Power BI, Python libraries (Matplotlib, Seaborn)
- Qualitative Data Analysis Software: NVivo, Atlas.ti, MAXQDAData Analysis Process Prepare Data: Clean, organize, and transform data as needed.
- Choose Appropriate Analysis Techniques: Select methods based on your research questions and data type.
- Apply Analysis Techniques: Use statistical software or other tools to analyze the data.
- Interpret Findings: Draw conclusions based on the results of your analysis.

**QUANTITATIVE DATA ANALYSIS:**

This focuses on numerical data, which is analyzed statistically to identify patterns or relationships. Summarizes the main features of a dataset. Measures of central tendency (mean, median, mode), measures of dispersion (variance, standard deviation, range).

**Example:** Finding the average age of participants in a survey.

**1. Inferential Statistics**

**Purpose:**

Draws conclusions from a sample to generalize to a population.

**Tools:** T-tests, chi-square tests, ANOVA, regression analysis, correlation analysis.

**Example:** Testing if there's a significant difference in sales before and after a marketing campaign.

**2. Data Visualization:**

Helps interpret and present data clearly.

**Tools:** Graphs, charts, and plots (e.g., bar charts, pie charts, scatter plots, histograms).

**Example:** Using a line graph to show a trend in product sales over time.

**Tools for Quantitative Analysis:**

**Software:** Excel, SPSS, SAS, R, Python (with libraries like Pandas, NumPy, Matplotlib, and Scikit-learn).

**Procedures:** Data cleaning, performing statistical tests, visualizing results, and interpreting them in context.

**QUANTITATIVE DATA ANALYSIS:**

Qualitative data is non-numerical and is analyzed to identify patterns, themes, and insights from text, audio, or video.

**1. Thematic Analysis:**

Identifies recurring themes or patterns within the data.

**Procedure:**

Coding data, grouping similar codes into themes, interpreting themes to answer research questions.

**Tools:** Manual coding or software like NVivo, ATLAS.ti, Dedoose.

**2. Content Analysis:**

Quantifies and analyzes the presence of certain words, phrases, or concepts in qualitative data.

**Procedure:** Breaking down text into categories, coding the frequency of specific elements, analyzing patterns.

**Tools:** NVivo, Excel for coding, specialized content analysis software.

**3. Narrative Analysis:**

Examines stories or personal accounts to understand how people construct meaning from events.

**Procedure:** Breaking down narratives, looking for key events, characters, and outcomes.

**Tools:** Manual analysis or qualitative software.

**4. Discourse Analysis:**

Studies communication (spoken or written) to understand social, political, or cultural context.

**Procedure:** Analyzing language use, identifying discourse patterns, and interpreting their implications.

**Tools:** Qualitative software or manual review.

**MIXED-METHODS DATA ANALYSIS**

This approach combines quantitative and qualitative analysis to provide a comprehensive understanding of the data.

**Concurrent Analysis:**

Analyzing quantitative and qualitative data simultaneously and integrating the results.

**Sequential Analysis:** One set of data is analyzed first (e.g., quantitative), followed by the other (e.g., qualitative) to build upon the findings.

**Tools:** NVivo (supports both qualitative and quantitative data), Dedoose, and statistical software for quantitative analysis

**Data Analysis Workflow**

1. **Data Cleaning:**

Identify and correct errors, handle missing values, and remove outliers.

**2. Exploratory Data Analysis (EDA):**

Gain initial insights through descriptive statistics or visualizations before formal analysis.

**3. Data Transformation:**

Convert data into a usable format (e.g., normalizing, coding qualitative data).

**4. Statistical or Thematic Analysis:**

Perform the appropriate analysis based on the type of data and research objectives.

**5. Interpretation and Reporting:**

Draw conclusions from the results, explain the findings, and relate them to the research questions.

**ADVANTAGES OF DATA ANALYSIS**

- Data analysis provides valuable insights that can inform better decision-making processes.

- By identifying trends and patterns, data analysis can help optimize operations and reduce costs.
- Data analysis can help identify root causes of problems and develop effective solutions.
- Data analysis can uncover new opportunities for growth and innovation.

**Disadvantages of Data Analysis**

- Poor quality data can lead to inaccurate and misleading results.
- Data analysis can raise privacy and security concerns, especially when dealing with sensitive personal information.
- Data analysis can be complex and requires specialized skills and tools.

**To maximize the benefits of data analysis and minimize its drawbacks, it is essential to:**

- Collect accurate and reliable data.
- Choose the right tools and methods for the specific analysis.
- Avoid overinterpretation and consider the limitations of the data.
- Present results in a clear and concise manner.
- Stay updated with the latest data analysis techniques and tools.

These guidelines, organizations can leverage the power of data analysis to gain valuable insights and drive positive outcomes.

# THIRTY-SEVEN
# INTERPRETATION

Interpretation section, the focus will be on making sense of the analyzed data by connecting the findings to the research questions and the existing body of literature. The quantitative results will be examined to identify significant trends and correlations, providing insights into the relationships among variables. For instance, if the survey results indicate a strong correlation between specific demographic factors and participants' attitudes, this will be discussed in relation to previous studies that highlight similar patterns or discrepancies.

Qualitative findings from interviews and focus groups will be interpreted to uncover deeper meanings and contextual factors influencing participants' responses. Thematic insights will be explored in light of theoretical frameworks established in the literature review, allowing for a richer understanding of the participants' experiences and motivations.

**Key Elements of Interpretation:**

**Restating Key Findings:**

Begin by summarizing the main findings of your analysis, but avoid repeating data verbatim. Highlight what the results mean in a simplified manner.

**Example:** "The data shows a 20% increase in customer satisfaction following the implementation of the new feedback system".

**Contextualizing the Results:**

Compare the findings with existing research, theories, or expectations.Discuss whether the results align with, differ from, or contribute new insights to previous studies.

Example: "This finding supports previous research by Smith (2020) but contrasts with the findings of Jones (2019), suggesting that customer feedback systems may vary in effectiveness depending on industry.

**Explaining the Implications:**

Discuss what the findings imply for the problem being addressed.

How does it contribute to solving the issue, and what are the practical applications?

Example: "The improvement in customer satisfaction indicates that implementing regular feedback loops can significantly enhance service quality in e-commerce platforms.

**Addressing Limitations:**

Acknowledge any limitations of your study, such as sample size, data collection methods, or external factors that could have influenced the results.

Example:

"Although the results are promising, the study's reliance on self-reported data may introduce bias, and future research should incorporate a broader demographic to validate these findings.

**Making Recommendations:**

Based on your interpretation of the results, provide actionable recommendations for stakeholders, such as further research areas, process improvements, or policy changes.

**Example:** "To further improve customer experience, we recommend implementing additional customer touchpoints through automated surveys at critical stages of the purchase journey.

**Linking Back to Objectives:**

Show how the findings address the initial research objectives or questions posed in the introduction of the report.

**Example:**

"The results clearly demonstrate that the new inventory management system has led to a reduction in order fulfillment time, which was one of the primary objectives of this study.

**Speculating on Future Trends:**

You may speculate on the potential future impact of your findings or how they could influence broader trends or innovations.

**Example:** "As automation in feedback collection becomes more sophisticated, we expect businesses to shift towards real-time customer service enhancements based on predictive insights.

**STRUCTURE OF THE INTERPRETATION SECTION:**

1. Introduction to Interpretation: Provide a brief overview of what the section will cover.

2. Summary of Key Findings: Highlight the most significant results and their direct meanings.

3. Contextual Analysis: Compare with literature, expectations, or industry norms.

4. Implications: Discuss the broader impact of the results on the field, organization, or problem.

5. Limitations: Acknowledge any constraints or limitations of the study.

6. Recommendations: Offer practical recommendations based on the findings.

7. Conclusion: Wrap up by linking findings to the research goals and suggesting next steps or areas for further research.

**Example:**

**Interpretation Section in a Project Report on E-Commerce Customer Satisfaction:**

The results of the customer satisfaction survey revealed a significant 20% increase in satisfaction levels following the implementation of the new feedback system. This suggests that customers appreciate the opportunity to provide input and feel that their concerns are being heard and addressed. Similar studies, such as Smith (2020), have also found that increased interaction through feedback mechanisms can foster customer loyalty. However, the findings diverge from Jones (2019), who suggested that feedback systems may lead to diminishing returns if overused.

These findings imply that the company's approach to integrating customer feedback is highly effective in improving service quality.

While the increase in satisfaction is clear, the study was limited by a focus on customers who made repeat purchases within three months of the initial contact. Future research should explore the impact of feedback collection on first-time buyers.

In terms of practical applications, the company should consider expanding the feedback system to other customer touchpoints, such as during the checkout process or after product delivery. This may further enhance satisfaction and provide valuable insights into customer behavior.

**Tips for Effective Interpretation**

- Avoid personal biases and subjective interpretations.

- Use evidence from your data to support your interpretations.
- Acknowledge any limitations of your research.
- Use clear and concise language to explain your findings.
- Don't make broad statements based on limited data

**Example of Interpretation Research Question:**

Does studying abroad improve students' language skills? Finding: Students who studied abroad scored significantly higher on a language proficiency test than students who did not.

Interpretation:

The findings suggest that studying abroad can be an effective way to improve language skills. This may be due to the immersive language environment that students experience abroad, which can provide opportunities for intensive language practice.

# THIRTY-EIGHT

# FINDINGS

The findings section in a project report presents the key results obtained from the data collection and analysis. This section is purely factual and objective, highlighting the most important outcomes without interpretation or explanation. The goal is to clearly present the data or results that directly address the research questions or objectives of the project.

**Key Components of the Findings Section:**

**1.Introduction:** Provide a brief introduction to the section, stating that it contains the key results derived from the data analysis.

**Example:** "The following section outlines the major findings from the data analysis conducted as part of this project.

**2. Presentation of Results:** Present the results systematically, often in the order of the research questions or objectives. For quantitative data, use tables, charts, graphs, and statistical results. For qualitative data, include excerpts from interviews, summaries of themes, or relevant qualitative evidence.

**Example (Quantitative):** "The survey responses indicated that 75% of customers rated the product quality as 'excellent,' with an overall satisfaction score of 4.5 out of 5.

**3. Use of Visual Aids:** Integrate charts, graphs, and tables where necessary to help clarify the data. Visual aids should be well-labeled and referenced within the text.

**Example**: "As shown in Figure 1, sales increased by 30% in the first quarter following the new marketing strategy implementation.

**4. Directly Linked to Objectives:**

Ensure that the findings directly correspond to the research questions or hypotheses posed in the introduction. Each finding should answer a specific objective.

**Example:** "Objective 1 was to evaluate customer satisfaction levels after the product launch. The survey results showed that satisfaction increased by 15% compared to pre-launch feedback.

**5. Avoid Interpretation:** The findings section should not contain explanations, implications, or opinions. These will be covered in the interpretation or discussion section.

**Example:** "The data shows a decline in user engagement over time, with a 10% drop in interaction rates after the second week. However, the reasons for this are addressed in the discussion section.

**6. Reporting Unexpected Findings:**

If unexpected or contradictory results arise, include them objectively in the findings section.

**Example:** "Contrary to expectations, the introduction of a loyalty program did not significantly impact repeat purchases, as only 5% of users took advantage of it.

**Example-Structure for a Findings Section:**

1. Customer Satisfaction Levels Survey responses indicate a significant improvement in customer satisfaction following the implementation of the new feedback system. Overall satisfaction rose by 20%, with 80% of respondents rating their experience as "excellent" (Figure 1).The net promoter score (NPS) increased from 55 to 68 within six months, reflecting improved customer loyalty.

2. Sales Performance Post-Marketing CampaignSales increased by 25% in the three months following the launch of the targeted digital marketing campaign (Table 1). The highest growth was observed in the 18-24 age group, which accounted for 40% of the increase.Conversion rates from website visitors to buyers rose from 3.5% to 5.2% in the same period.

# THIRTY-NINE

# LIMITATIONS

The limitations section in a project report acknowledges the weaknesses or constraints encountered during the research or project process. It is important because it demonstrates transparency and helps readers understand the context in which the findings should be interpreted. Addressing limitations also adds credibility to the report, as it shows that you are aware of factors that could affect the results or conclusions.

**Components of the Limitations Section:**

1. **Scope of the Study:**

Clearly define the scope of the research or project, which may inherently limit the generalizability or comprehensiveness of the findings.

**Example:** "This study focused on customer satisfaction in a single retail chain, limiting the ability to generalize findings to the broader retail industry.

**2. Sample Size and Composition:** Discuss any issues with the sample size or representativeness of the participants. A small or biased sample could limit the applicability of the findings.

**Example:** "The sample size was limited to 50 participants, which may not accurately represent the entire population of customers using the service.

**3. Data Collection Methods:**

Address limitations related to the tools or techniques used to collect data. This might include the accuracy, reliability, or completeness of the data.

**Example:** The reliance on self-reported data from surveys may introduce response bias, as participants might have provided socially desirable answers.

**4. Time Constraints:**

Time limitations can affect the depth and breadth of the project. Discuss how time constraints may have restricted the study.

**Example:**

Due to time constraints, the study was conducted over a three-month period, which may not capture long-term trends or behaviors.

**5. External Factors:**

Mention any external or environmental factors that could have influenced the results but were beyond your control.

**Example:** "Market conditions during the research period were unusually volatile due to economic uncertainties, which may have affected consumer purchasing behavior.

**6. Technological or Resource Limitations:**

If there were limitations in the tools, technologies, or resources available, explain how these affected the project.

**Example:** "The project was limited by the available software, which could not track real-time customer interactions, potentially missing critical data.

**7. Limitations in Analysis:**

Discuss any challenges or limitations in the methods of data analysis, including statistical power or qualitative coding methods.

**Example:**

"Due to the complexity of the data, a simplified regression model was used, which may not fully capture the nuances of customer behavior.

**8. Subjectivity and Bias:**

In qualitative research or areas involving human judgment, acknowledge any potential biases or subjectivity in the data interpretation process.

**Example:** "The thematic analysis was conducted by a single researcher, which may introduce personal bias into the interpretation of the qualitative data.

**Example of a Limitations Section:**

a. Limitations Despite the promising findings of this study, several limitations must be acknowledged. First, the study was conducted over a relatively short time frame of three months, which may not fully capture long-term trends in customer satisfaction.
q. Additionally, the sample size of 100 participants, though sufficient for initial insights, is not large enough to ensure the generalizability of the

results to the broader population.

q. The reliance on self-reported survey data also poses a potential limitation. Participants may have provided socially desirable responses, rather than honest opinions, which could introduce response bias.

# FORTY
# RECOMMENDATIONS

The recommendations section of a project report provides practical and actionable suggestions based on the findings and conclusions of the study. This section aims to offer ways to address the issues identified, improve processes, or guide future research. Recommendations should be directly linked to the report's findings and presented clearly to inform decision-makers or stakeholders on the next steps.

1. **Link to Findings:**

Each recommendation should be rooted in the findings or conclusions of the project. Avoid introducing new ideas or suggestions that were not part of the analysis.

Example: "Based on the finding that customer service response times negatively impacted satisfaction, we recommend increasing the number of support agents during peak hours.

**2. Actionable Suggestions:**

Recommendations should be specific and practical, offering clear steps that can be implemented. Vague or overly general recommendations are less useful.

Example:

"Implement a live chat feature on the website to provide real-time support, reducing the average response time from 15 minutes to under 5 minutes.

**3. Prioritize Recommendations:** If there are multiple recommendations, consider prioritizing them by importance, feasibility, or potential impact. This helps decision-makers know where to focus efforts.

**Example:**

"Priority 1: Enhance the website's user interface for easier navigation;

Priority 2: Expand the product return policy to accommodate international customers.

**4. Consider Feasibility:**

Address the feasibility of each recommendation in terms of resources, time, and budget. Recommendations should be realistic and consider any constraints the organization may have.

Example: "Given the current budget constraints, we recommend beginning with a pilot program in one region before expanding customer service improvements across all locations.

**5. Short-Term vs. Long-Term:**

Differentiate between recommendations that can be implemented quickly (short-term) and those that require more time or resources (long-term). This helps in planning and execution.

Example: "In the short term, increase email support capacity by hiring two additional agents. In the long term, develop an AI-powered chatbot to handle frequent inquiries.

**6. Justify the Recommendations:**

Support each recommendation with evidence from the findings and explain why it is beneficial or necessary.

Example: "We recommend optimizing the website's mobile version, as the data shows that 60% of users access the site through mobile devices, yet the bounce rate is 35% higher than on desktops."

# FORTY-ONE
# CONCLUSION

**Conclusion** section, the primary aim is to succinctly summarize the key findings and their implications while reinforcing the significance of the study. This section will begin by restating the research objectives and briefly outlining how they have been addressed through the data analysis and interpretation. Key insights from both the quantitative and qualitative analyses will be highlighted, emphasizing any notable trends, correlations, or themes that emerged from the research.

The conclusion will also reflect on the contributions of the study to the existing body of literature, discussing how it fills identified gaps and advances understanding in the field. Additionally, the practical implications of the findings will be considered, suggesting how they can inform practice, policy, or future research initiatives.

Limitations acknowledged in earlier sections will be revisited to provide a balanced perspective on the findings, suggesting that while the study offers valuable insights, there are areas that require caution in interpretation. Finally, the conclusion will end with a call for further research, pointing to specific areas or questions that warrant additional exploration. By summarizing the study's contributions and outlining future directions, this section will reinforce the overall significance of the research and its potential impact on both theory and practice.

# FORTY-TWO

# BIBLIOGRAPH

The bibliography (or reference list) in a project report is a section that lists all the sources (books, articles, websites, reports, etc.) that were consulted and cited throughout the report. This section is important because it gives credit to the authors of the works you used, demonstrates the breadth of research, and allows readers to locate the sources for further investigation.

**Key Elements of the Bibliography:**

1. **Citing All Sources:**

Every source you referred to in your research must be included in the bibliography.

**These may include:**

a. Books
q. Journal
q. Articles
q. Websites
q. Reports
q. Conference
q. papers
q. Databases

**Example of Bibliography Entries in Different Styles:**

1. APA Style: Book: Smith, J. A. (2020). Data analysis for beginners. New York, NY: Academic Press. Journal Article: Johnson, M. L. (2019). The

impact of technology on customer satisfaction. Journal of Business Research, 45(3), 101-115.Website:Anderson, B. (2022, June 12). How AI is transforming customer support. Retrieved from https://www.technews.com/ai-customer-support

2. Chicago Style: Book: Smith, John A. Data Analysis for Beginners. New York: Academic Press, 2020.Journal Article: Johnson, Mary L. "The Impact of Technology on Customer Satisfaction." Journal of Business Research 45, no. 3 (2019): 101-115.Website:Anderson, Bill. "How AI Is Transforming Customer Support." TechNews. June 12, 2022. Accessed August 10, 2023. 4. IEEE Style: Book: J. A. Smith, Data Analysis for Beginners, New York, NY, USA: Academic Press, 2020.

**Journal Article:**

3. M. L. Johnson, "The impact of technology on customer satisfaction," J. Bus. Res., vol. 45, no. 3, pp. 101-115, 2019.Website:B. Anderson, "How AI is transforming customer support," TechNews, June 12, 2022. [Online]. Available:https://www.technews.com/ai-customer-support.

**General Guidelines for Bibliography:**

**Check for Completeness:** Ensure each reference includes all necessary information (author, title, year, etc.).

**Keep the Format Consistent:** Ensure all references follow the same citation style.

**Proofread:** Double-check spelling, punctuation, and formatting for each entry.

**Include Only Cited Sources:** Make sure that every source in the bibliography was cited in the report.

**Tips:** Use reference management tools like Zotero, Mendeley, or EndNote to help organize citations and generate formatted bibliographies. Refer to the specific style guide (APA, MLA, Chicago, IEEE, etc.) for detailed instructions on formatting unusual sources, such as interviews or social media posts. By providing a well-structured bibliography, you give proper credit to the original authors and provide readers with a pathway to explore your sources further.

# FORTY-THREE

# PROOF READING A REPORT

Proofreading is a crucial step in the writing process. It involves carefully reviewing a document to identify and correct errors in grammar, punctuation, spelling, and formatting. A well-proofread report reflects professionalism and enhances the credibility of the writer.

**Key Steps in Proofreading:**

1. **Take a Break:**
    - Step away from your writing for a short period. This allows you to return with a fresh perspective.
2. **Read Aloud:**
    - Reading your work aloud can help you identify awkward phrasing, missing words, and other errors.
3. **Check for Grammar and Punctuation:**
    - Use grammar and spell-check tools, but also rely on your own judgment.
    - Pay attention to comma usage, apostrophes, and subject-verb agreement.
4. **Verify Facts and Figures:**

- ◦ Ensure that all facts, figures, and citations are accurate and consistent.
- ◦ Cross-reference with original sources.

5. **Review Formatting and Style:**

    - ◦ Check for consistency in fonts, font sizes, and spacing.
    - ◦ Ensure that headings, subheadings, and paragraphs are formatted correctly.
    - ◦ Adhere to the specified style guide (e.g., APA, MLA, Chicago).

6. **Check for Clarity and Coherence:**

    - ◦ Ensure that your writing is clear, concise, and easy to understand.
    - ◦ Check for logical flow and coherence between paragraphs and sections.

7. **Seek Feedback:**

    - ◦ Ask a colleague, friend, or mentor to review your work.
    - ◦ Consider joining a writing group to receive feedback from peers.

**Common Mistakes to Watch Out For:**

- Typos and Spelling Errors: Use spell-check and proofreading tools to identify and correct these mistakes.
- Punctuation Errors: Pay attention to comma usage, apostrophes, and quotation marks.
- Grammar Errors: Ensure that sentences are grammatically correct and that subject-verb agreement is accurate.
- Word Choice: Use precise and appropriate language. Avoid using clichés and jargon.
- Sentence Structure: Vary sentence structure to avoid monotony.
- Paragraph Structure: Ensure that each paragraph has a clear topic sentence and supporting details.
- Formatting and Style: Adhere to the specified formatting guidelines and maintain consistency throughout the document.

## THE IMPORTANCE OF PROOFREADING A REPORT

Proofreading is a crucial step in the writing process that ensures the quality and professionalism of your report. Here are some of the key benefits of proofreading:

**1. Enhanced Credibility:**

- A well-proofread report reflects professionalism and attention to detail.
- Error-free writing builds trust with your readers.

**2. Clear and Effective Communication:**

- Proofreading helps to identify and eliminate unnecessary words and phrases.
- It ensures that ideas are presented in a logical and coherent manner.

**3. Improved Reader Experience:**

- A well-proofread report is easier to read and understand.
- Clear and concise writing keeps readers engaged.

**4. Error Prevention:**

- Proofreading helps to identify and correct these common errors.
- It ensures that your writing is grammatically correct.

**5. Adherence to Style Guidelines:**

- Proofreading helps to ensure consistency in formatting, citation style, and other stylistic elements.
- It helps to meet the specific requirements of academic writing.

# FORTY-FOUR

# AVOIDING TYPOGRAPHICAL ERRORS

Typographical errors can significantly diminish the credibility of your project report. To ensure accuracy and professionalism, consider these tips:

1. Proofread Carefully:

- This helps you catch errors that might be overlooked when reading silently.
- Utilize software like Grammarly or Microsoft Word's built-in tools to identify and correct errors.
- Ensure consistent formatting, font styles, and spacing throughout the document.

2. Seek Feedback:

- Ask colleagues or classmates to review your work for errors.
- Consider hiring a professional editor for a thorough review.

3. Take Breaks:

- Step away from your work for a short period to return with a fresh perspective.
- Frequent breaks can help reduce eye strain and improve focus.

4. Use Spell-Check and Grammar-Check Tools:

- These tools can identify common errors, but remember to proofread manually as well.

5. Pay Attention to Detail:

- Carefully review each sentence and paragraph.
- Ensure that references and citations are accurate and consistent.
- Verify that formatting, font styles, and spacing are consistent throughout the document.

6. Be Mindful of Common Errors:

- Be aware of words that sound similar but have different meanings (e.g., their, there, they're).
- Use commas, semicolons, and periods correctly to separate independent clauses.
- Ensure that subjects and verbs agree in number.
- Make sure pronouns agree with their antecedents.

# FORTY-FIVE
# BIBLIOGRAPHY IN REQUIRED FORMAT

A bibliography is a list of sources cited in your research. It's essential to include a bibliography in your project report to give credit to the original authors and to allow readers to verify the information you've presented.

**Common Citation Styles**

The specific format for your bibliography will depend on the style guide required by your institution or the journal you're submitting to. Some common citation styles include:

- **APA (American Psychological Association):** Widely used in social sciences and humanities.
- **MLA (Modern Language Association):** Commonly used in humanities and language arts.
- **Chicago/Turabian:** Used in history, literature, and other humanities fields.
- **Vancouver:** Used in medical and scientific fields.

**Key Elements of a Bibliography Entry**

Regardless of the style guide, a typical bibliography entry includes the following elements:

- **Author's Name:** Last name, first name (or initials).
- **Title of the Work:** Italicized for books and articles, quotation marks for shorter works.

- **Publication Information:** Publisher, publication date, journal title, volume number, issue number, page numbers, etc.
- **DOI (Digital Object Identifier):** A unique identifier for digital objects.
- **URL (Uniform Resource Locator):** The web address of the source.

**Example of APA Style Bibliography Entry:**
**For a Book:**

- Author, A. A. (Year). *Title of book.* Publisher.

**For a Journal Article:**

- Author, A. A., Author, B. B., & Author, C. C. (Year). Title of article. *Journal Name, Volume Number*(Issue Number), pages. [invalid URL removed]

**For a Website:**

- Author, A. A. (Year, Month Day). Title of page. Website Name. URL

**Tips for Creating a Bibliography**

- Tools like Zotero, Mendeley, or EndNote can help you organize your sources and generate citations in the correct format.
- Follow the specific guidelines provided by your institution or department.
- Ensure that all information is accurate and consistent.
- Pay attention to formatting details like font, spacing, and indentation.
- Refer to a style guide like the APA Publication Manual or the MLA Handbook for detailed instructions.

# FORTY-SIX

# FONT

The choice of font in a project report significantly impacts its readability and overall presentation. Here are some key considerations when selecting a font:

**1. Readability:**

- Opt for fonts that are easy to read, such as Times New Roman, Arial, or Calibri.
- Avoid script or cursive fonts as they can be difficult to read, especially in smaller font sizes.

**2. Professionalism:**

- Choose fonts that convey a professional and academic tone.
- Maintain consistency throughout the document.

**3. Visual Appeal:**

- Balance the font choice with the overall design and layout of the report.
- Use bold, italic, or larger font sizes to emphasize important points.

**4. Accessibility:**

- Consider using fonts like Open Dyslexic or Arial Black, which are designed to be more readable for individuals with dyslexia.

**Specific Font Recommendations:**

- **Body Text:**
    - Times New Roman (12pt)
    - Arial (11pt)
    - Calibri (11pt)
- **Headings and Subheadings:**
    - Larger font size (e.g., 14pt or 16pt)
    - Bold or italic formatting
- **Citations and References:**
    - Smaller font size (e.g., 10pt)

**CONSIDERATION:**

- Stick to a limited number of fonts to maintain a clean and consistent look.
- Choose a font that is appropriate for your audience.
- Use bold, italic, and underline sparingly to emphasize key points.
- Ensure that the font choice does not interfere with the readability of your document.

## SPACING

Proper spacing is crucial for enhancing the readability and overall presentation of your project report. Here are some key considerations for spacing:

**Line Spacing**

- **Main Body Text:** Typically, 1.5-line spacing is used for the main body text. This spacing provides adequate white space between lines, improving readability.
- **Headings and Subheadings:** Use double-spacing between headings and subheadings to create visual hierarchy.
- **Paragraph Spacing:** Add an extra line space between paragraphs to separate ideas and improve the overall flow of the document.

### Margins

- **Standard Margins:** Use standard margins of 1 inch on all sides (top, bottom, left, and right). This provides ample space for binding and printing.
- **Adjustments:** In some cases, you may need to adjust the margins slightly to accommodate specific formatting requirements or to optimize the layout.

### Alignment

- **Left Alignment:** Left-align the text for a clean and professional look.
- **Justified Alignment:** Avoid justified alignment, as it can create uneven spacing and make the text harder to read.

### Tables and Figures

- **Spacing Around Tables and Figures:** Ensure that there is adequate spacing around tables and figures to separate them from the main text.
- **Caption Placement:** Place captions above tables and below figures.
- **Alignment:** Align tables and figures to the center of the page for a balanced layout.

# FORTY-SEVEN

# CHECKING TABLES AND ILLUSTRATIONS

Tables and illustrations are valuable tools for presenting data and information visually in a project report. However, it's essential to ensure their accuracy, clarity, and consistency. Here are some key points to consider when checking tables and illustrations:

**1. Accuracy and Consistency:**

- Double-check all data points to ensure accuracy.
- Maintain consistent formatting for tables and figures throughout the report.
- Use consistent units of measurement (e.g., metric or imperial).

**2. Clarity and Readability:**

- Provide clear and concise titles and captions for each table and figure.
- Label all axes, columns, and rows appropriately.
- Use a clear and readable font size and style.
- Use color coding strategically to highlight specific information.
- Choose appropriate chart types (e.g., bar charts, line charts, pie charts) to effectively represent the data.

**3. Relevance:**

- Ensure that each table and figure directly supports the text.
- Avoid presenting the same information in multiple formats.

**4. Placement:**

- Place tables and figures near the relevant text to improve readability.
- Refer to tables and figures in the text to guide the reader.

**5. Formatting:**

- Align tables and figures to the center of the page or to the left margin.
- Ensure adequate spacing between tables and figures and the surrounding text.
- Use appropriate line weights for table borders and figure lines.

**6. Citation:**

- If the table or figure is adapted from another source, cite the source appropriately.
- If necessary, obtain permission to reproduce copyrighted material.

# FORTY-EIGHT

# PRESENTING A REPORT ORALLY

Presenting a report orally is a skill that can significantly impact the effectiveness of your communication. Here are some key tips to help you deliver a compelling and informative presentation:

**1. Understand Your Audience:**

- Determine the knowledge level, interests, and expectations of your audience.
- Adjust your content and style to suit your audience's needs.

**2. Structure Your Presentation:**

- **Introduction:**
    - Grab the audience's attention with a strong opening statement or question.
    - Briefly outline the main points of your report.
    - Clearly state the main argument or purpose of your presentation.
- **Body:**
    - Organize your content into clear and concise main points.
    - Use data, statistics, and examples to support your claims.
    - Ensure a smooth and logical progression of ideas.

- **Conclusion:**
    - Recapitulate the main points of your presentation.
    - Restate your thesis statement in a powerful way.
    - Encourage the audience to take action or consider a specific viewpoint.

**3. Use Effective Visual Aids:**

- Create visually appealing slides that complement your presentation.
- Avoid cluttering slides with too much text.
- Incorporate images, charts, and graphs to enhance understanding.
- Rehearse your presentation with your slides to ensure smooth transitions.

**4. Practice Your Delivery:**

- Practice your presentation multiple times to build confidence and fluency.
- Ensure that your presentation fits within the allotted time.
- Use body language effectively to engage your audience (e.g., eye contact, gestures, posture).
- Vary your tone, pace, and volume to maintain audience interest.

**5. Handle Questions Effectively:**

- Pay attention to the question and ask for clarification if needed.
- Pause before answering to gather your thoughts.
- Provide direct and concise answers.
- Even if you don’t know the answer, be polite and offer to follow up.

# FORTY-NINE
# TECHNIQUES

A well-structured and well-written project report is essential for conveying research findings clearly and concisely. Here are some techniques to enhance your project report writing. Use clear and concise language, avoiding jargon and technical terms that may be unfamiliar to your audience. Structure your report logically, using headings and subheadings to guide the reader. Employ visual aids like charts, graphs, and diagrams to enhance understanding and engagement. Present data accurately and effectively using tables and figures. Analyze data critically and draw meaningful conclusions. Adhere to ethical guidelines and ensure data integrity. Carefully proofread your report to eliminate errors in grammar, punctuation, and spelling. Share your draft with peers or supervisors for constructive feedback. Cite all sources accurately and consistently using a recognized style guide (e.g., APA, MLA, Chicago). Use a consistent format throughout the report, including font, font size, line spacing, and margins.

Effective project report writing is a crucial skill for researchers, students, and professionals alike. By following the guidelines outlined in this book, you can create clear, concise, and well-structured reports that effectively communicate your findings. Remember to prioritize clarity, organization, and accuracy in your writing. Use a consistent format, pay attention to detail, and proofread carefully. By adhering to these principles, you can produce high-quality project reports that leave a lasting impression.

As technology continues to evolve, it's important to stay updated with the latest tools and techniques for project report writing. Embrace digital tools and online resources to enhance your writing process. Ultimately, the goal of a project report is to convey information clearly and persuasively. By following the guidance provided in this book, you can achieve this goal and produce exceptional reports that contribute to your academic or professional success.

# FIFTY

# QUESTION BANK

## Unit I

**Writing Skills – Essential Grammar and Vocabulary – Passive Voice, Reported Speech, Concord, Signpost words, Cohesive Devices – Paragraph writing - Technical Writing vs. General Writing.**

**1.What is passive voice?**

Passive voice emphasizes the action itself rather than who performed it. (e.g., "The report was written" - emphasizes the report being written)

**2.What are two situations where using passive voice might be appropriate in writing?**

- To emphasize the action: When you want to draw attention to the action itself rather than who performed it.

Example: "The new product was launched successfully this week." (Focuses on the launch itself)

- When the doer is unknown: If you don't know who or what performed the action.

Example: "A mistake was made during the data entry process." (Unknown who made the mistake)

**3.What is reported speech?**

Reported speech allows you to convey someone else's words while maintaining a consistent writing style. (e.g., "The CEO said the company is growing." - reports the CEO's words)

**4.How can reported speech be used in PR writing?**

Reported speech can be used to convey information from experts or external sources while maintaining a clear writing style in PR materials.

**5.List three types of cohesive devices used to connect sentences within a paragraph.**

Three types of cohesive devices used to connect sentences within a paragraph are:

1. **Conjunctions:** These are words that join sentences or clauses, such as "and," "but," "because," and "so."
2. **Pronouns:** These refer back to nouns previously mentioned in the paragraph, avoiding repetition and creating a smoother flow. (e.g., "The car was red. **It** had a dent on the fender.")
3. **Transition words:** These words or phrases signal relationships between ideas, helping the reader transition from one thought to the next. Examples include "however," "furthermore," "in addition," and "consequently.

**6.Define the term "subject-verb agreement" in the context of writing.**

Subject-verb agreement in writing refers to the grammatical rule that ensures the subject (who or what performs the action) and the verb (the action itself) match in number (singular or plural).

- **Singular subject:** Requires a singular verb. (e.g., The cat **jumps** over the fence.)
- **Plural subject:** Requires a plural verb. (e.g., The cats **jump** over the fence.)

**7.Why is subject-verb agreement important?**

Subject-verb agreement avoids confusion about who/what performs the action, improving sentence clarity.

**8.Name one example of a signpost word used for contrasting viewpoints.**

- Conversely

This word indicates an opposing idea or conclusion.

**9.What is the main difference between technical writing and general writing in terms of audience?**

The main difference between technical writing and general writing in terms of audience is their level of knowledge and expertise:

- **Technical writing:** Targets a specific audience with specialized knowledge of the subject matter. It uses technical terms and assumes some understanding of the field.
- **General writing:** Targets a wider audience with a general level of knowledge. It uses more common language and avoids overly technical terms.

**10. Explain how proper concord (subject-verb agreement) contributes to sentence clarity?**

Proper subject-verb agreement is crucial for sentence clarity because it ensures the reader immediately understands who or what is performing the action.

- **Avoids Confusion:** When the subject and verb disagree, the sentence becomes grammatically incorrect. This creates confusion for the reader as it's unclear who/what is meant.
- **Identifies the Doer:** Proper agreement clarifies who or what is responsible for the action in the sentence. This improves readability and makes the intended meaning clear.

**For example:**

- **Incorrect:** The cars drive by quickly. (Plural subject with singular verb)
- **Correct:** The cars drove by quickly. (Plural subject with plural verb - clarifies multiple cars are driving)

**11.Describe the role of signpost words in structuring paragraphs.**

Signpost words signal transitions between ideas, helping readers navigate the flow of information.

**12.In what way can reported speech be used effectively in PR writing?**

Reported speech in PR writing effectively conveys expert opinions (quotes/paraphrases) while maintaining a clear and consistent writing style, boosting message credibility and audience understanding.

**13.Explain the importance of clear and concise writing in PR materials for effective communication?**

- **Grabs Attention & Boosts Retention:** Clear, concise messages hook readers and ensure they remember the key takeaway. Complex sentences or jargon get lost in the shuffle.
- **Reaches a Wider Audience:** PR materials target diverse audiences. Clear writing avoids technical terms, making the message accessible to everyone.
- **Builds Credibility & Trust:** Clear, professional writing reflects well on the organization, fostering trust with the audience – essential for PR success.

**Drives Action:** Concise writing emphasizes the call to action, whether it's a website visit or brand recall, maximizing engagement.

**14.Differentiate between a paragraph written for technical writing and one for general writing in terms of vocabulary.**

| Feature | Technical Writing | General Writing |
|---|---|---|
| Vocabulary Level | Precise, specialized terms | Common language |
| Examples | Microcontroller, ADC | Tiny computer chip, data acquisition |
| Assumed Knowledge | Reader has some prior knowledge of the subject | Reader has no specific knowledge of the subject |
| Explanation of Jargon | Not always provided | Explained within context or avoided altogether |
| Goal | Clarity for a specific audience | Clarity for a wider audience |

Enter Caption

**15.What are cohesive devices?**

**Cohesive devices** are words or phrases that connect sentences within a paragraph, improving the flow and overall structure.

- Conjunctions

- Pronouns
- transition words

**16. Explain the concept of target audience in writing.**

The specific group of people you are writing for, which influences your style and vocabulary.

**17. List two essential elements of good technical writing.**

- Accuracy
- Clarity

**18. Why is it important to use transition words in your writing?**

Transition words are the secret weapon of strong writing. They seamlessly connect sentences, guiding readers through your ideas. Without them, your writing can feel like a confusing maze. But transition words do more than create flow. They signal connections between ideas, highlighting contrasts ("however") or emphasizing key points ("moreover"). This strategic use builds a unified message, ensuring readers grasp your argument. In short, transition words are essential for clear and impactful writing.

**19. Explain the role of strong verbs in effective writing?**

Strong verbs play a key role in effective writing by:

- Painting a clearer picture to add action and energy, making your writing more vivid and engaging.
- They convey the action more precisely, leaving less room for misinterpretation.
- Strong verbs grab the reader's attention and keep them engaged with the text.

**20. How can the active voice make your writing more engaging?**

Active voice breathes life into your writing. It prioritizes clarity by placing the acting subject upfront, eliminating confusion about who's doing what. Strong verbs take center stage, adding action and dynamism to your sentences. This focus on the "doer" and the action itself creates a more engaging experience for the reader.

## UNIT II

**Project Report – Definition, Structure, Types of Reports, Purpose – Intended Audience – Plagiarism– Report Writing in STEM fields –**

**Experiment – Statistical Analysis.**

**1.What is a project report?**

A project report is a comprehensive document that details the objectives, methodology, results, and outcomes of a project. It serves as a formal record that communicates the project's journey, findings, and conclusions to stakeholders.

**2.Briefly outline the typical structure of a project report.**

The typical project report structure includes an introduction, literature review (STEM fields), methodology, results, discussion, conclusion, and references.

1. **What are the different types of project reports?**

Different types of project reports include

- Feasibility reports (assessing project viability)
- Progress reports (updating on project development)
- Final reports (summarizing the entire project).

1. **When would you use a progress report versus a final report?**

Use a progress report to provide updates on ongoing projects, while a final report is used to present the completed project's findings and conclusions.

5. **Why do we write project reports?**

We write project reports to document the project's journey, communicate findings, and gain approval or inform stakeholders.

- Transfer knowledge for future projects to learn from past experiences.
- Evaluate success by comparing results to goals and informing future decisions.

6. **Who is the intended audience for a project report?**

The intended audience for a project report depends on the project. Project reports target various audiences. The core audience project managers, team members, funders needs detailed info, while a broader audience senior management, clients, public might be interested in a high-level summary or the project's impact.

7. **Define plagiarism in your own words.**

Plagiarism is basically stealing someone else's work and pretending it's your own. It can involve copying their words directly, or even just their ideas without giving them credit. It's like taking someone else's homework and saying you did it yourself, which isn't fair or honest.

1. **Why is plagiarism a serious issue in academic and professional writing?**

Plagiarism is serious because it undermines academic integrity and devalues original work.

- Dishonesty and Lack of Originality
- Misrepresentation and Unreliable Information

9. **How does report writing differ in STEM fields compared to other disciplines?**

Report writing in STEM fields emphasizes clarity, precision, and objectivity, focusing on data and analysis compared to other disciplines.

10. **Explain the importance of clear and concise language in STEM reports.**

In STEM reports, clear and concise language is essential for accuracy and efficiency.

- Accuracy: Precise wording avoids confusion and ensures findings are communicated clearly. Jargon or overly technical terms can misrepresent complex data.
- Efficiency: A concise report allows readers to grasp key points quickly, saving time and ensuring accurate interpretation of the research.

**11. What is the role of an experiment in a STEM project report?**

The experiment plays a central role in a STEM project report by acting as the testing ground for the project's hypothesis. It describes the:

- Methods: How the experiment was conducted, including materials, procedures, and steps taken.
- Data Collection: How the data was gathered during the experiment (e.g., measurements, observations).

**12. Why is statistical analysis often used in STEM reports?**

- Statistical methods identify patterns and trends within the data, revealing relationships that might not be obvious at first glance.
- Statistics help assess the strength and validity of the results. They tell us if the observed effects are likely due to the experiment or simply random chance.
- Based on the analysis, we can draw more reliable conclusions about the experiment and its implications.

**13. When might you use visuals (graphs, charts) in a report?**

- Simplify complex data: Visuals can present large amounts of data in a clear and easily digestible way, making it easier to identify trends and patterns.
- Highlight key findings: Charts and graphs can draw attention to important results, allowing readers to quickly grasp the main points.
- Enhance understanding: Visuals can make abstract concepts more concrete and easier to remember for readers.

**14. Explain the importance of interpreting your data in a report?**

A well-structured project report, with clear explanations and concise language, guides the reader through the project's journey, from objectives to impactful conclusions.

15. **In your own words, describe the key steps involved in writing a project report?**

Writing a project report involves outlining your goals, explaining how you achieved them, presenting the results, and explaining what it all means.

You'd then wrap it up with clear conclusions and any recommendations for the future.

16. **Give an example of a situation where a project report would be required?**

Imagine part of a team developing a new phone app to help users learn language. After months of work, built and tested the app. A project report would be required to document the entire process:

- Initial goals and features planned.
- Methods used for development and testing.
- User feedback and data collected.
- The app's final functionalities and effectiveness.

17. **How can you ensure your report is free from plagiarism?**

- Always cite your sources whenever you paraphrase or directly quote someone else's work. Use a consistent citation style (APA, MLA, etc.) throughout your report.
- While referencing is important, aim to understand the source material and then rephrase the ideas in your own words. This demonstrates your comprehension and avoids simply copying.

18. **Why is it important to tailor your report to its intended audience?**

A project report's effectiveness hinges on tailoring it to its audience, ensuring clarity, relevance, and impactful communication for informed decisions.

## UNIT III

**Structure of the Project Report: (Part 1) Framing a Title – Content – Acknowledgement – FundingDetails -Abstract – Introduction – Aim of the Study – Background - Writing the research question -Need of the Study/ Project Significance, Relevance – Determining the feasibility – Theoretical Framework.**

**1. What is the role of a title in a project report?**

A good title should be clear, concise, and accurately reflect the project's content.

**2. What is the purpose of the acknowledgement section in a project report?**

The acknowledgement section recognizes individuals or organizations that provided support or assistance during the project.

**3. What type of information might be included in the funding section of a project report?**

The funding section details the sources and amounts of financial support received for the project.

**4. What is the purpose of an abstract in a project report?**

The abstract provides a concise summary of the entire report, including the research question, methods, key findings, and conclusions.

**5. What is the main objective of the introduction section in a project report?**

The introduction sets the context for the project by introducing the research topic, background information, and the overall purpose of the study.

**6. What does the "Aim of the Study" section in a project report typically address?**

This section clearly states the specific objectives or goals that the research aims to achieve.

**7. What is the purpose of including background information in a project report?**

The background section provides relevant context and existing knowledge related to the research topic, highlighting the need for further investigation.

**8. What is a research question and how is it formulated?**

A research question is a specific, focused inquiry that guides the investigation and defines what the project aims to answer or explore. It should be clear, concise, and researchable.

1. **Why is it important to explain the need for your study in a project report?**

Explaining the need or significance of your study justifies its importance and convinces the reader why this research is worth conducting.

10. **What does "relevance" mean in the context of a project report?**

Relevance refers to the importance and applicability of your research findings to a specific field or audience.

11. **What does determining the feasibility of a project involve?**

Feasibility assessment evaluates if the project can be realistically completed within the available resources time, budget, personnel and with the chosen methods.

12. **What is a theoretical framework in a project report?**

A theoretical framework outlines the underlying theories or concepts that guide your research and provide a lens for interpreting your findings.

13. **What information might be included in the methodology section of a project report?**

The methodology section describes the research methods used to collect and analyze data, including participant selection, data collection techniques, and data analysis procedures.

14. **What is the purpose of the results section in a project report?**

The results section presents the findings of your research in a clear and organized manner, often using tables, figures, and charts to support your findings.

15. **What does the discussion section in a project report typically focus on?**

The discussion section interprets the results, explains their significance in relation to the research question and background information, and discusses potential limitations or implications of the findings.

16. **What are some ethical considerations that researchers should address in a project report?**

Ethical considerations might include

- informed consent
- participant confidentiality
- data privacy
- responsible research practices.

17. **What is the main purpose of the conclusion section in a project report?**

The conclusion section summarizes the key findings of the research, restates the research question, and highlights the overall contribution of the study to the field.

18. **What does the "future directions" section in a project report typically address?**

This section suggests potential areas for further research based on the findings of the current study.

19. **What types of information might be included in the appendices of a project report?**

Appendices can contain detailed data tables, additional figures, lengthy questionnaires, or other supplementary materials that support the main content of the report but might disrupt the flow of the main text.

20. **What are some advantages of using appendices in a project report?**

Appendices allow researchers to include detailed information that might be too cumbersome for the main body of the report while still making it accessible to readers who are interested in the specifics.

## UNIT IV

Structure of the Project Report: (Part 2) – Literature Review, Research Design, Methods of Data Collection - Tools and Procedures - Data Analysis - Interpretation - Findings –Limitations - Recommendations – Conclusion – Bibliography.

1. **What is the purpose of a literature review in a project report?**

A literature review summarizes existing research related to your topic, identifying relevant theories, studies, and findings to provide context and demonstrate your awareness of the field.

1. **What does "research design" refer to in a project report?**

Research design outlines the overall strategy for conducting your research, including the type of study (e.g., experimental, survey) and the methods used to collect and analyze data.

3. **What are some examples of data collection methods used in research projects?**

- Data collection methods can include surveys, questionnaires, interviews, observations, experiments, and document analysis.
- The chosen method depends on the research question and the type of data needed.

**4. What does it mean to "analyze data" in a project report?**

Data analysis involves organizing, processing, and interpreting the collected data to identify patterns, trends, or relationships relevant to your research question.

5. **What is the difference between "findings" and "interpretation" in a project report?**

- Findings are the raw data or results obtained from your research.
- Interpretation explains the meaning of these results, drawing connections to your research question and existing knowledge.

6. **Why is it important to acknowledge limitations in a project report?**

Acknowledging limitations demonstrates transparency and helps readers understand the potential weaknesses or constraints of your study, leading to a more nuanced interpretation of the findings.

7. **What are "recommendations" in the context of a project report?**

Recommendations suggest potential future research directions or actions based on the findings of your study. These recommendations can be for further investigation, practical applications, or improvements to existing practices.

8. **What is the main purpose of the conclusion section in a project report?**

The conclusion section summarizes the key findings and their significance, reiterates the research question and objectives, and highlights the overall contribution of the study to the field.

9. **What information might be included in the bibliography of a project report?**

The bibliography lists all the sources you cited in your report, providing proper references for the information used in your research.

10. **Why is a literature review important before starting your own research?**

- A literature review prevents duplication of effort, builds on existing knowledge, and helps you refine your research question.
- It strengthens research and proposal.

11. **What are some factors to consider when choosing a data collection method?**

- Choosing a data collection method involves considering the research question's data needs.
- desired data type.
- practicality factors like time, cost, and participant access.

12. **What tools and procedures might be used for data collection?**

Data collection tools and procedures vary based on method:

- surveys (online platforms/questionnaires)
- interviews (recording devices/interview guides)

- observations (field notes/checklists)
- experiments (lab equipment/specific protocols)
- document analysis (existing documents/coding for themes).

**13. How can data visualization be helpful in a project report?**

- Lines connect data points, revealing trends and how data changes over time.
- Unlike points that just mark positions, lines show the overall direction and progression of your project.
- Lines help paint a clearer picture, making it easier to follow the narrative of your project's development.

**14. What are some ethical considerations when interpreting research findings?**

- Be aware of bias
- Explain limitations
- Consider generalizability
- Focus on evidence strength
- Report all findings honestly.

15. **Why should the findings section be presented in a clear and organized way?**

- clarity ensures readers grasp the study's key results.
- Organization helps readers follow the data's story, making it easier to understand trends and patterns.
- Clarity allows readers to effectively interpret the findings in the context of your research questions.

16. **What are some examples of limitations a researcher might acknowledge in a project report?**

- Discuss sample limitations
- Method influences
- Data challenges
- How time/cost constraints affected your research.

17. **How can recommendations make your research more impactful?Conclusion and Beyond ?**

- They translate your findings into actionable steps, guiding readers on how to apply research in real-world settings.
- Recommendations demonstrate the practical significance of your research, making it more relevant to policymakers, practitioners, or the public.
- Well-defined recommendations can motivate stakeholders to implement changes or pursue further research based on findings.
- Recommendations can outline potential areas for future research, inspiring others to build upon work and advance knowledge in the field.

18. **How does a strong conclusion connect the findings back to the research question?**

- Restating the research question.
- Summarizing key findings
- Highlighting the findings answer and the question.

19. **What is the difference between a bibliography and a reference list?**

- **Reference list:** Includes only sources directly cited in work.
- **Bibliography:** Lists all sources consulted, even if not directly cited.

20. **What are some benefits of using proper citation methods in a project report?**

- Credibility
- Transparency
- Avoids Plagiarism
- Strengthens Arguments

## UNIT V

**Proof reading a report – Avoiding Typographical Errors – Bibliography in required Format – Font –Spacing – Checking Tables and Illustrations – Presenting a Report Orally – Techniques.**

**1. What is the importance of using a consistent font style and size in a professional report?**

Using a consistent font style and size improves readability and creates a professional appearance for your report. It allows readers to focus on the content without distractions caused by varying fonts or sizes.

1. **Why is it important to check the bibliography in a report?**

A well-formatted bibliography ensures proper credit is given to the sources you used in your research. This strengthens the credibility of your report and allows readers to find the original sources for further information.

1. **Why is it important to avoid typographical errors and grammatical mistakes in a report?**

Typographical errors and grammatical mistakes can distract readers from the content and create a negative impression of your professionalism. A polished report with clear writing demonstrates your attention to detail and strengthens the overall impact of your work

3. **What's the benefit of using clear and concise language when presenting a report orally?**

Clear and concise language in an oral presentation makes it easier for the audience to understand your message. They can follow your points more readily, retain key information, and stay engaged throughout your talk.

4. **Briefly describe two different techniques for checking for typographical errors in a report.**

- **Proofreading:** This involves carefully reading your report multiple times, preferably on paper and in a well-lit environment. Focus on individual words, checking for typos, grammatical errors, and punctuation mistakes.
- **Spell Check and Grammar Tools:** Utilize built-in spell checkers and grammar tools in your word processing software. However, rely on these as aids, not replacements, for thorough proofreading as they may miss

certain errors.

5. **What are some key considerations when choosing an appropriate font for a professional report?**

- **Readability:** The primary consideration is choosing a clear and easy-to-read font like Times New Roman, Arial, or Calibri. Avoid decorative or hard-to-decipher fonts.
- **Professionalism:** Opt for a font commonly used in professional settings. Avoid overly casual or trendy fonts that may appear less formal.
- **Consistency:** Maintain consistency by using the same font throughout the report, including headings, body text, and captions.

6. **Why is it important to maintain consistent spacing throughout your report?**

- Proper spacing between lines, paragraphs, and sections improves visual distinction and helps readers differentiate between different elements of the report.
- Consistent spacing creates a professional appearance, making the report more visually appealing and less cluttered.
- Adequate spacing prevents text from appearing crammed or overwhelming, allowing readers to comfortably navigate the content.

7. **Explain the concept of "active voice" and how using it can improve the clarity of your report's writing style**

- **Directness:** It puts the subject (who performs the action) at the beginning of the sentence, leading to a more straightforward and engaging writing style.
- **Focus on the Actor:** Active voice highlights who is responsible for the action, improving clarity and reducing ambiguity.
- **Conciseness:** Active voice tends to be more concise than passive voice, using fewer words to convey the same information and enhancing readability.

**9. How does the use of spell-check and grammar check tools aid in avoiding typographical errors?**

- Spell-check and grammar check tools significantly aid in avoiding typographical errors by automatically identifying and suggesting corrections for misspelled words, grammatical mistakes, and punctuation errors.
- These tools act as a first line of defense, helping to catch common mistakes that might be overlooked during manual proofreading.
- Additionally, they can offer suggestions for improving sentence structure and word choice, enhancing overall document quality

**10. Explain the importance of consistency in formatting to prevent typographical mistakes.**

- Consistency in formatting is crucial for preventing typographical mistakes as it establishes a clear and predictable visual structure for the document.
- When fonts, font sizes, spacing, and other formatting elements are consistent, it becomes easier to identify errors and inconsistencies.
- This reduces the chances of overlooking typos, as deviations from the established format often stand out, making them readily apparent.
- A uniform appearance also enhances readability and professionalism.

**11. Why is it essential to maintain a consistent bibliography format throughout a report?**

1. Consistency in bibliography format enhances readability and professionalism. A uniform style helps readers easily locate and identify sources, improving the overall presentation of the report.

2. Maintaining a consistent bibliography format demonstrates attention to detail and academic rigor. It shows that the author has carefully researched and cited sources according to established standards.

**12. Name two common bibliography styles used in academic writing.**

1. APA (American Psychological Association): Commonly used in social sciences, psychology, and education.

2. MLA (Modern Language Association): Primarily used in humanities fields like literature, language studies, and cultural studies.

**13. How does appropriate font size and style contribute to the readability of a report?**

- 1. Appropriate font size enhances readability by ensuring the text is easily legible.
- 2. Font style impacts readability by influencing the overall appearance and tone of the report.

**14. What is the standard line spacing recommended for formal reports?**

- 1. Standard line spacing for formal reports is typically 1.5 lines or double-spaced. This spacing improves readability by providing ample white space between lines, making the text easier to follow.
- 2. Consistency in line spacing throughout the report is essential. Variations in spacing can disrupt the visual flow and make the document appear unprofessional.

**15. Why is it crucial to verify the accuracy of data presented in tables and illustrations?**

- To maintain credibility and reliability: Accurate data forms the backbone of a project report. Errors or inconsistencies can undermine the report's credibility and lead to incorrect conclusions.
- To support sound decision-making: Decisions made based on inaccurate data can have serious consequences. Verifying data ensures that the information used for analysis and recommendations is reliable and trustworthy.

**16. How can you ensure that tables and illustrations are properly labeled and captioned?**

1. Use clear and concise titles and captions that accurately reflect the content of the table or illustration.
2. Ensure labels are placed close to the corresponding elements within the table or illustration for easy reference.

**17. What is the significance of using visual aids during an oral presentation?**

**Improving audience comprehension:** Visuals help to clarify complex information and make it easier for the audience to understand key points.

**Enhancing engagement:** Visuals can capture and maintain audience attention, making the presentation more interesting and dynamic

**18. Mention two effective techniques for engaging the audience during a report presentation.**

Interactive elements: Incorporate questions, polls, or group activities to involve the audience directly and encourage participation. This keeps them actively engaged and helps to gauge their understanding.

Storytelling: Weave a narrative into the presentation by sharing personal anecdotes or real-life examples related to the report's content. This helps to connect with the audience on an emotional level and make the information more relatable.

**19. What is the significance of proofreading a report before submission?**

**1. Enhances credibility and professionalism:** A well-proofread report free from errors reflects positively on the author and the organization, conveying a professional image.

**2. Improves clarity and understanding:** Proofreading helps to eliminate ambiguities, typos, and grammatical mistakes, ensuring that the report's message is conveyed accurately and effectively.

**20. Mention two common typographical errors that can be rectified during proofreading.**

Spelling errors: Incorrectly spelled words can significantly impact readability and comprehension. Proofreading helps identify and correct these mistakes.

Punctuation errors: Incorrect use of commas, periods, apostrophes, and other punctuation marks can alter the meaning of sentences. Careful proofreading ensures proper punctuation usage.

www.ingramcontent.com/pod-product-compliance
Ingram Content Group UK Ltd.
Pitfield, Milton Keynes, MK11 3LW, UK
UKHW041637190726
13854UKWH00006B/2542

9 798896 106395